PRAISE FOR

The 6 Reasons You'll Get the Job

"Once again, Debra and Elisabeth deliver! *No One Is Unemployable* became a Top Ten Career Book of the Year by giving job seekers who face tough barriers genuine hope and effective practicality. *The 6 Reasons You'll Get the Job* is great because it reveals to the rest of us how people really get jobs. Insightful, smart, and fun to read! I rate this book a 'Buy Now.'"

—Joyce Lain Kennedy, syndicated columnist, Tribune Media Services

"As a former employer, I am impressed with the research and insight that went into this book. I wish I'd had it when I was interviewing and hiring people for my company. The authors have it right! Readers will learn to think like the employers they want to work for. They will gain the confidence and focus needed to present themselves as applicants that employers want to pursue. A lot of employers and a wide variety of job seekers will benefit from this."

—Rich Van Hattem, cofounder and vice president (retired), $5.5 billion company with 30,000 employees

"There's only one reason to read this book: Debra and Elisabeth tell you exactly what you need to know to get hired."

—Tory Johnson, CEO, Women For Hire

"Finally, a job search book that teaches people to think like the employer. More people would be getting hired faster if every job seeker in America understood what this book teaches—that they are hired to make the company successful, that it's not just about their ability but their overall fit for the company, and that they must make the company more than they cost. If you're already working, this book can help you keep your job and advance your career."

—Joel Manby, featured on CBS's *Undercover Boss*, CEO of Herschend Family Entertainment Corporation

continued . . .

"If you want to change your luck in the job search, read this book! It reveals insightful secrets and strategies to positively position yourself at the head of the pack." —Susan Whitcomb, author, *Résumé Magic*

"A glut of job search and career books floods the market, but most repeat the same information or lack research-backed authority. Finally, MacDougall and Sanders-Park have brought a fresh, new, authoritative perspective to this saturated world of job search advice—including that on the Internet. Their six reasons model challenges job seekers' long-held, but ineffective, practices. Giving employers what they really want seems like such an obvious concept, but candidates rarely grasp the employer's perspective. All that is poised to change with this revolutionary book. It's a must for the bookshelf of anyone who ever expects to look for a job."

—Katharine Hansen, PhD, associate publisher and creative director,
Quintessential Careers

"A great new look at an old topic! As always, Deb and Elisabeth give clear, accurate advice. Whether you are white collar or blue, this book offers you lots of great, practical tips."

—Richard Knowdell, executive director, Career Development Network,
and author, *Building a Career Development Program*

"In today's highly competitive job market, it's more important than ever to understand how to position yourself as the perfect match to the hiring company's needs. In this book, Debra and Elisabeth hit the nail right on the head!" —Craig Karasin, president, CareerSuccessions.com

"Many job seekers are on overdrive in today's very tough job market. What they need are real-world, creative ideas that can be put into action now. Elisabeth and Debra have written the one book that offers true insight and impact so many of us need—and they have done it all in a style that is easy and breezy to read. Masterful and magical!"

—Jerri Rosen, CEO and founder, Working Wardrobes

"They're right! You have to think like the employer, and ability alone will not get you hired . . . Luckily, they tell you what will. I've seen the principles of this book in action. They work, and they'll get work for you."

> —**David Mills, nationally known trainer and how-to book author**

"Practical wisdom, whimsical expression, and realistic and doable strategies on how to job search and be the employee an employer will keep, promote, and delight in having on their team. Debra and Elisabeth know the 'how-to' of getting the career you dream of and breaking the 'just get a job' mentality."

> —**Shirley Shackleford, national director of adult development,**
> **Here's Life Inner City**

"The degree gets college grads in the hunt . . . but *The 6 Reasons You'll Get the Job* gets them the prize! I'd hand college students this gem with their diploma."

> —**Rich Feller, PhD, professor and University Distinguished**
> **Teaching Scholar, Colorado State University**

Debra Angel MacDougall
Elisabeth Harney Sanders-Parks

The 6 Reasons You'll Get the Job

*WHAT EMPLOYERS LOOK FOR—WHETHER
THEY KNOW IT OR NOT*

Foreword by Richard Bolles, author of
What Color Is Your Parachute?

PRENTICE HALL PRESS

PRENTICE HALL PRESS
Published by the Penguin Group
Penguin Group (USA) Inc.
375 Hudson Street, New York, New York 10014, USA
Penguin Group (Canada), 90 Eglinton Avenue East, Suite 700, Toronto, Ontario M4P 2Y3, Canada
(a division of Pearson Penguin Canada Inc.)
Penguin Books Ltd., 80 Strand, London WC2R 0RL, England
Penguin Group Ireland, 25 St. Stephen's Green, Dublin 2, Ireland
(a division of Penguin Books Ltd.)
Penguin Group (Australia), 250 Camberwell Road, Camberwell, Victoria 3124, Australia
(a division of Pearson Australia Group Pty. Ltd.)
Penguin Books India Pvt. Ltd., 11 Community Centre, Panchsheel Park, New Delhi—110 017, India
Penguin Group (NZ), 67 Apollo Drive, Rosedale, North Shore 0632, New Zealand
(a division of Pearson New Zealand Ltd.)
Penguin Books (South Africa) (Pty.) Ltd., 24 Sturdee Avenue, Rosebank, Johannesburg 2196,
South Africa

Penguin Books Ltd., Registered Offices: 80 Strand, London WC2R 0RL, England

While the author has made every effort to provide accurate telephone numbers and Internet addresses
at the time of publication, neither the publisher nor the author assumes any responsibility for errors
or for changes that occur after publication. Further, the publisher does not have any control over and
does not assume any responsibility for author or third-party websites or their content.

First edition: October 2010

Library of Congress Cataloging-in-Publication Data

MacDougall, Debra Angel.
  The 6 reasons you'll get the job : what employers look for—whether they know it or not / Debra
Angel MacDougall, Elisabeth Harney Sanders-Parks ; foreword by Richard Bolles.
    p.   cm.
  Includes bibliographical references and index.
  ISBN 978-0-7352-0476-8
  1. Job hunting. 2. Applications for positions. 3. Vocational guidance. I. Sanders-Parks,
Elisabeth Harney. II. Title. III. Title: Six reasons you will get the job.
  HF5382.7.M313   2010
  650.14—dc22   2010021227

PRINTED IN THE UNITED STATES OF AMERICA

10 9 8 7 6 5 4 3 2 1

Most Prentice Hall Press books are available at special quantity discounts for bulk purchases for sales
promotions, premiums, fund-raising, or educational use. Special books, or book excerpts, can also
be created to fit specific needs. For details, write: Special Markets, Penguin Group (USA) Inc., 375
Hudson Street, New York, New York 10014.

Dedicated to the thousands of job seekers and employment professionals who have proven that these techniques work, and to those of you looking for work—may the tools and hope you find here help you find a job and keep you employed for as long as you choose.

Acknowledgments

We are incredibly passionate about the work we do, and we are thankful for the support we have gotten over the years from partners around the world and for their help in bringing this book to life. Thank you . . . to the employers and industry experts we have worked with and learned from over the years, and to those who invested their time in reviewing our manuscript: Gill Tulloch, Rodney Halstead, David Cowie, Keith Winters, Gordon MacDougall, Brian Sanders-Park, Gretchen Maswadeh, Dale Susan Brown, Denise Bissonnette, and Jennifer Repo. To the Margret McBride Literary Agency and our agent, Donna Degutis, who believed in us and this project from the beginning, and to the Prentice Hall Press publishing team and our extremely talented editor, Maria Gagliano, for her extraordinary guidance in making this book a reality. To our mentor, Richard Bolles, for his faithful guidance over the years, and to our husbands and families for their unwavering support. To God for His love, His grace, and the opportunity to serve people in such a powerful and meaningful way.

Contents

Foreword

I am always on the lookout for interesting people who then decide to write a book.

Because, generally speaking, if they are interesting, their book will be, too.

I found one of these interesting people in the person of Deb Angel, who is one of the two authors of this book. When I met her, she was leading a seminar at a careers conference that I have attended routinely for many years, mostly because they invited me back to be the keynote speaker year in and year out. At the conference, I'd prowl the halls long before and long after it was my turn to speak. All kinds of job-hunting seminars would be going on, and I would drop in on one, listen for a while, then go see if something more interesting was happening in another room, farther down the hall.

What was I looking for? Well, I've already said it: interesting people. But, more than that: new ideas. Interesting, innovative, and helpful new ideas.

I had a peculiar handicap in this search: I was an author myself, and in fact, my book was the first bestseller in the field of job hunting or career changing, thus kindling publishers' interest and sparking their search for other titles that they could publish in this field. By the time I blundered into Deb's seminar, my book, revised annually, had already sold millions of copies around the world, and there were now literally thousands of career books out there, when there had only been twelve when I first began. Over the years my ideas had been copied by so many authors, many of whom didn't even know where the ideas came from, that the careers editor at the *San Francisco Chronicle* once wrote: "If Dick's ideas were removed from the thousands of careers books that are out there, we would be left with a very small library indeed."

Well, this summation is all very nice for my ego, but that's not why I'm telling you this. I want you to understand that when I was eavesdropping on one job-hunting seminar after another, looking for new ideas, I was handicapped because I kept hearing what were primarily my own ideas, in one form or another, again and again. But then, one wonderful day, I dropped in on Deb Angel's seminar. And I was astonished! I heard one new idea after another, from Deb and her teaching partner, Elisabeth Harney. I started scribbling like mad, jotting down one new helpful idea after another. It was the most rewarding day I ever spent at that particular conference.

So, I had found my "interesting person." Naturally I talked with her and later had lunches with her and Elisabeth, then I befriended them and tried to learn as much as I possibly could from both of them. They had written a book. I devoured it.

When I heard these interesting people were writing a new book, I begged to write the foreword. And here it is. I can't tell you strongly enough how highly I think of Deb and Elisabeth. Or how much I think you will profit from reading any book, and most particularly this one, written by these interesting women. If you're out of work, or working with those who are, or if you are interested in the so-called forgotten marginal people who most job-hunting counselors and the media never talk about, then you simply must read this book.

Incidentally, I do know that Deb married a careers man, brilliant and famous in his own right in Scotland, and so her legal last name isn't Angel anymore; it's MacDougall. (I was, after all, at Gordon and Deb's wedding at St. Andrews in Scotland.) But I still like to think of her as Deb Angel. After you've read what she and Elisabeth have written, and most especially if you've been "hangin' on the ropes" and these ideas rescue you, you may think of her as an angel, too.

Dick Bolles
April 8, 2010

Introduction

Do you want to know the real reason employers aren't hiring you? They won't tell you, but they tell us. For more than twenty years, through bad economic times and good, we've been helping people get good jobs. Along the way, we've been asking employers why they do and don't hire people. Because they don't have to worry about hurting someone's feelings or getting sued, they can be brutally honest with us. And we're here to be honest with you.

So, what's holding you back? You might be surprised to discover that it's not just the economy, or your personal barriers. Every day thousands of people start new jobs, and you only need one! In fact, during the worst part of the recent recession, 4.3 million Americans were hired in a single month.[1] And for every barrier you have, there is someone who has faced it, overcome it, and is working today. If they can do it, we know you can, too! Choose a positive mind-set from the start, because what you believe matters. As Henry Ford said, "Whether you think you can or can't, you're usually right."

Over the years we've discovered two key things that hold our clients back. The first is not realizing that talent alone rarely gets you hired. Usually the candidates on the final short list all have the ability to do the job, so the deciding factor is something more. That "more" can be found in the six areas employers scrutinize, consciously or subconsciously, when deciding who to hire and who to screen out. If you view them from the employer's perspective, everything that is holding you back and every strength that will get you hired can be found in these six areas: presentation, ability, dependability, motivation, attitude, and network. Each area sounds familiar enough, but as we explain them you may be surprised at how employers judge them. The second thing that holds people back is the fear of doing things differently from everyone else. The rational side of our brain says we need to job search the way everyone else does—look for advertisements in the Open Job Market and submit dozens of résumés or applications each day. Yet experience shows that it doesn't work. Chances are, that's not how you landed your last job and it doesn't seem to be working for you now. Perhaps it's time to try something new. The fastest way to get a job is to stand out from the crowd, rather than follow it. That's where we come in.

This book will challenge many of your beliefs about job searching. It will teach you how to step into the employers' shoes, so you can discover and remove all the reasons you're getting screened out, and prove you are the ideal candidate for *their* job. It will teach you how to find side doors that lead directly to decision makers, while your competition is still waiting in the lobby. And, before we're done, we'll even show you how to get hired for a job you've never been paid to do. In these pages, you'll meet many of the people we have helped—from professionals, to skilled labor-ers, to first-time job seekers—and see how they got hired. Their goals and barriers may be similar to yours or very different, but what led to their success can get you hired, too. As you read their stories, look past any differences to the techniques and concepts being taught. As we share the insider information we've gained over twenty years, notice how it renews your confidence so you can face your fears and execute a job search that turns the reasons you're not getting hired into the six reasons you'll get the job.

PART 1

The Real Reasons
You're Not Getting Hired

We're going to let you in on the employers' perspective, starting with the six reasons they do and don't hire. All employer needs and concerns can be grouped into six major areas:

Presentation

Ability

Dependability

Motivation

Attitude

Network

(PADMAN, for easy reference)

These are the six reasons you will get the job, or the very reasons you won't! They may sound obvious, except that employers think about them differently than most of us do. Thinking like an employer is critical to establish control of your job search, because the employer decides who gets screened out and who gets hired. As you begin to look at your job search from the employer's perspective, you begin to notice the issues they face every day. In the next two chapters, we'll teach you to see yourself through their eyes, so you can craft a job search strategy that removes everything holding you back and deliberately highlights your strengths in each area of PADMAN, so you get hired.

Seeing yourself through the employers' eyes is not the only way to bring their perspective into your job search. You can incorporate proven business methods to get in front of employers (your "customer") and "sell" your qualifications. Oddly, even very capable businesspeople often rely on the least effective methods when marketing themselves in the job search. We all know that mass mailings have a very low rate of return—it's called junk mail for a reason. Even personalized or targeted, they're not nearly as effective as a personal sales pitch from someone who believes in the product—particularly for big-ticket items that cost thousands of dollars a year—like new employees. So what does this mean for your job search? It means that mailing out dozens of résumés and hoping an employer will "buy" you is a long shot. If you tailor your résumé to the job and industry, your chances improve. If you address correspondence directly to the decision maker, you increase your odds even more. But to significantly improve your chances of making a quick sale, use a side door technique we teach to persuade employers to request your résumé. First, let's take a look at the employer's perspective of the hiring process so you can use it to your advantage.

☞ TAKING A PAGE FROM BUSINESS . . .

Effective marketing campaigns always start with a *key message*. In job search, it's your top two or three accomplishments or qualities that you want repeated when your name comes up—*He's the one who had us all laughing. His track record shows he's a fast study and usually exceeds targets . . . She's the one with the Harvard MBA who secured over $4 million in funding for the XYZ project.* Make it something the employers need but may not find or notice in other applicants. Use this proven technique in all your marketing efforts—résumés, cover letters, spontaneous letters, interviews, and side door meetings. Throughout your job search, repeat it in several different ways so employers remember it.

1

Thinking Like Everyone Else Can Keep You Unemployed

Before we explore how thinking like an employer can get you hired, let's look at how thinking like everyone else can keep you unemployed. In bad economic times, employers who are hiring abandon the Open Job Market—where jobs are advertised to the general public—for the Hidden Job Market—where jobs are not advertised. That's one of the reasons you see fewer jobs posted in newspapers and trade magazines, and on the Internet and job boards. Employers do this because listing jobs in the Open Market brings a flood of applicants they don't have the time or staff to sort through. We heard a story recently about a small home insulation business in a less populated part of the country that was awarded a new contract and needed seven new employees. They advertised in the local paper and arranged to hold the interviews at a nearby hotel. They expected about fifty applicants—more than two hundred were in line before they even began. By noon, more than five hundred people had applied or were waiting to be interviewed. Imagine if you were that employer. The next time you needed more staff, you wouldn't put an ad in the paper, and neither would we.

In good economic times, it is estimated that about 20 percent of available jobs are advertised in the Open Market, and the remaining 80 percent are found in the Hidden Market.[1] In bad economic times, even fewer jobs are advertised. Yet, most job seekers (eight out of ten) search primarily in the Open Market. Clearly your chances are better in the Hidden Market, where you compete with only two applicants for eight jobs, rather than vying with eight people for two jobs in the Open Market. Using the Hidden Market can quadruple your odds of landing a job.

➥ DID YOU KNOW?

There are two ways to job search. The traditional method is to use the *front door* by submitting a résumé or application and hoping for an interview. The more effective method is to find a *side door* to the person with the power to hire and impress that person so that he or she requests your résumé. Using a side door does not refer to actually sneaking into a building; it's a metaphor for meeting and impressing the manger before they know you want a job. Both front door and side door approaches can be successfully used in the Open Market, but only side doors are truly effective in the Hidden Market.

Here are some ways to access jobs in the Hidden Market. Employers often ask their best employees if they know of anyone who would be good in the job. In fact, many companies give bonuses to staff who refer applicants who are hired. Employers believe that our friends are like us, so if we're good, our friends are likely to be, too. Plus, if you recommend a friend, you'll probably help them be successful. Employers also ask their family, friends, business associates, customers, suppliers, project partners, as well as fellow members of service clubs, associations, civic boards, community committees, and so on. Connections with these people can help you get hired because they can open side doors that lead directly to the person with the power to hire. So identify the industries or companies where you want to work, and list everyone you know, socially and professionally, who could introduce you to decision makers. Vendors who supply your industry (like a health inspector visiting local restaurants, or an office supply delivery driver) are a good source for job vacancies because they chat with staff from different companies every day and often hear who is laying off, short-staffed, or hiring.

Expand your list to include acquaintances. Picture this: You've become friendly with a parent of another player on your son's football team. During one of your regular Saturday morning chats, he asks about your work and tells you about his skills. Later, he mentions that your company seems like a good place to work and asks if you would introduce him to your manager. If you like him and think he would do well, you are likely to say yes. Sociologist Mark Granovetter's classic study found that more than 55 percent of job seekers saw their references only occasionally, and 28 percent saw them rarely.[2] In the book *The Tipping Point*, Malcom Gladwell agrees that studies show "people weren't getting jobs through their friends. They were getting them through their acquaintances."[3] So, you're likely to find your next job through someone you don't see often or know well.

You can also access the Hidden Market by proactively contacting employers directly. Most employers put off advertising new positions as long as they can, due to the cost and time involved. So making contact while they are in the "thinking about it" phase is often viewed as fate. After all, you have just saved them lots of time and money. Although you may not know who is "thinking about it," if you contact enough employers, you will find them. If you have specific companies you really want to work for and don't know anyone who can introduce you, instead of sending your résumé, try another side door such as a spontaneous letter (described in Chapter 5). It is more personal and targeted and, most important, will get better results than a mass-mail résumé.

In some industries, companies build trusted relationships with head hunters, employment agencies, university or trade school professors, and career center staff that only refer candidates who match their needs in the six vital areas. Other employers like to "try before they buy," so they use temp agencies and hire only the very best. In good economic times, for difficult-to-fill positions some employers even hire great people they don't need now but will need soon, because great employees are so hard to find. A final and often favored method of finding new employees is to poach them from other companies. So when you're working, treat every customer as a prospective employer so you land your next job while you are still employed.

➤ DID YOU KNOW?

Temp and employment agencies are a Hidden Market source for the employer, but in bad economic times they are an Open Market source for the job seeker because agencies can get hundreds of résumés for each job opening and are even more ruthless in their screen-out practices.

If you get temporary work through agencies that serve your industry, treat every moment of every assignment like an interview, so you get hired in-house.

Clearly, finding side doors into the Hidden Market is the most effective way to get a job, but the rational side of your brain may be saying, "Yeah, but . . ." It wants you to do what everyone else is doing, because familiarity feels safe. A colleague of ours shared a story about an unemployed executive who understood the value of looking in the Hidden Market. Yet, he spent 75 percent of his time searching in the Open Market. Once he landed a job, he stated that he always knew he would find his job using side doors in the Hidden Market, but that he wasted so much time on a traditional search because the rational side of his brain, and his wife, needed to be appeased.

Realizing the truth in the executive's statement, we will give you lots of tips on how to improve your chances in the Open Market. However, your best success will come in the Hidden Market. And that's our specialty. We'll show you how to direct as much time and effort as your rational brain will allow to finding side doors into the Hidden Market so you're hired more quickly.

The rational brain may also be thinking that the safest option is to give up. The nightly news, stories from other job seekers, and hearing nothing or a flat-out no in your job search can take its toll. You may no longer have the energy to turn off the news, seek out employed acquaintances to find out what worked for them, or begin a job search in the Hidden Market. We understand. In more than twenty years of helping people find work, we've learned how debilitating self-doubt and fear can be. The truth is, fear is so universal among job searchers that it's the norm. You may fear that no one will see your value and hire you, or wonder if you have value any longer. Perhaps you fear that you'll be rejected yet again, be seen as a failure by friends and family, or get stuck in a job you hate. Learning how to move through these fears is invaluable in your job search. The techniques in this book will work better if you deal with your fear along the way.

Often we aren't aware of our own fear. During a job search, fear rears its ugly little head in strange ways—insecurity, isolation, faking illness, or actually getting sick. Some people keep busy with other "important" activities, or use the kids, car, or the weather as an excuse not to search. Some sabotage real success by pursuing jobs they don't actually want, constantly change their job target, appear overconfident, or reject opportunities before they are rejected. Fear even manifests itself as hiding behind a computer rather than connecting with people, or sending lots of blind résumés instead of researching companies and tailoring your approach. What does your fear look like? What unhelpful actions and attitudes crop up when it's time to job search? Be honest with yourself. If you're not, your fear may make you feel depressed, angry, or tired, or cause you to overeat, drink too much, use drugs, aimlessly surf the web, or waste job search time. If you recognize your fear, you can devise a plan to deal with it.

⌦ TAKING A PAGE FROM BUSINESS . . .

The best boss I ever had used to say, "When you're feeling overwhelmed, just pick three things and do them. When they're done, pick three more." Three things always felt doable. To this day, I remain surprised at how much I can achieve following this simple rule.

There are two things that compel people to deal with their fear. The first is the negative result of remaining immobilized by fear. Take the case of Mel, who had accepted his first accounting job even before graduating from college, and had secured each new position while he was still employed. In his mid-fifties, his department was suddenly closed and everyone laid off. For the first time in his life, Mel was forced to job search while unemployed. He was gripped with fear, and hearing no to his initial efforts fed his fears that he was too old, that he would have to settle for less pay and prestige, or that no one would hire him at all. Job searching became such a scary, negative, and futile duty, he even thought of just calling it an "early retirement." But there was another dynamic in his life—his family. Mel couldn't bear the shame of telling his wife they would have to downsize their home, or his daughter she'd have to attend a state school instead of the private university that had just accepted her. Mel's fear was great, but the pain of staying unemployed was greater. It drove him to confront his fear and try something new. We taught him what this book will teach you. With this new information, Mel's confidence returned and so did the job offers.

The second reason people confront their fear is to achieve the life they desperately want but know won't happen until they face that fear. Betty Jo was a U.S. soldier who completed her tour of duty and was considering leaving the armed forces. She knew that many people in her family and town were unemployed. She hadn't done well in high school and worried that she couldn't provide for her daughter. Her family was encouraging her to stay in the military and continue sending money home. But she missed her daughter and really wanted to raise her. Plus, the army had instilled in her a confidence that she could learn, achieve her goals, and get help from others if she asked. Betty Jo's faith in herself and passion for being a hands-on mom compelled her to put aside her fear, investigate her options, and use her GI bill to attend nursing school once she left the service. She began volunteering at the hospital she most wanted to work for to demonstrate her positive attitude, build a professional network, and get help with her studies from her new mentors. Fourteen months later she completed her education, received her license, and was offered a job at the hospital. It's true that fear can keep us safe, but inaction can rob us of opportunities to live our dreams. Facing your fears and taking action is one of the bravest things you can do. It allows you to take control of your life and determine your future. What will compel you to face your fears about job searching in a new way? Consider these questions:

- What in your current situation is worse than job searching? What will happen if you don't begin working soon?
- What do you want your life to look like in six months, a year, or ten years? Is getting a job central in making it a reality?

If what you are doing now isn't giving you the life you want, it's time to try something new. Here are some tips for managing your fear:

- Get *new information* on how to job search in today's market. We'll give you lots of new ideas and techniques.
- Find places to get industry-specific information and news about your local market. Once the unknown is known, the mystery of job searching fades, and your fear will, too.
- Take *small steps* and celebrate your successes. Don't look at the job search as one big task—break it into smaller components. Start with the things you can do well, and give yourself credit.
- Have *realistic expectations*. Acknowledge that you will encounter companies that aren't hiring, just hired, are out of business, don't acknowledge you, or even interview you three times and then say "no thanks." Sales representatives will tell you that only one out of ten

potential customers will buy. So give yourself a break if you don't make a sale at your first interview. Evaluate it and determine how you can improve next time.

• Identify *role models*, people who have faced similar issues and succeeded, and do what they did. Throughout this book, we share lots of stories of people who got jobs despite their fears and other employment barriers.

• Finally, find an *accountability partner*, someone you can be honest with about your goals and fears, who cares enough to help you move forward. Spending time with someone who supports your dreams and believes in you is one of the most helpful things you can do.

Now that you know the value of trying something new and have some tools for quieting your fear, let's get started on getting you hired! As with any successful business venture the best place to start is with the customer. In the job search, the employers are your customer, so throughout this book we will teach you the employers' perspective, because they are the people you must impress to get hired.

2

The Hiring Process
Through the Employer's Eyes

So how do employers think? First, they don't think of themselves as "employers." If you ask a thousand people what they do for a living, no one is going to say, "I'm an employer." That's not even a job title! It's a function, and not always a welcome one. "Employers" see themselves as business owners, department managers, accountants, plumbers, retailers, and so on, who must employ people to increase their success. Most view dealing with employee-related issues—including hiring—as a distraction from their real jobs. They want to spend as little time as possible doing it. Yet most companies don't have a Human Resources (HR) Department or dedicated hiring manager. Instead, an assistant is given the added task of screening out applicants. So in your job search, you'll probably be dealing with very busy people who have lots of other things to do, who are already short-staffed, and who may not know a lot about hiring. The easier you make it for them to see your value, the easier it is for them to recommend you to the person with the power to hire. Even in companies that have HR, the person who makes the final hiring decision isn't in HR (unless you are going for a job in that department). The person with the power to hire you is almost always the company manager or your department head. In the Open Market, the assistant or the HR staff are your doorway to the decision maker, so treat them with respect.

➡ DID YOU KNOW?

It's not uncommon for an interviewer to have *not* reviewed your résumé before stepping into the interview. Don't assume they have. Repeat your key messages a couple of times as well as highlighting the other selling points that can get you hired.

Second, although the company has stated goals, each department manager also has a personal agenda. Like you and me, these managers are concerned about their own success. If they own the company, it's tied to the company's success and reputation. If they manage within the company, it's tied to their own job security or advancement potential. One surefire way to get hired is to prove you can help your manager achieve her goals. Managers are evaluated on both their personal effectiveness and the effectiveness of their team. They want team members who will help them get the job done, and make them look good. The more you know about your prospective manager, the better prepared you can be to prove you will help him achieve his goals.

➤➔ **DID YOU KNOW?**

Being good at the job is often not enough to get you hired if a manager perceives that you could cause problems or won't follow her lead.

Third, employers don't hire because they have a vacancy; they hire because they believe someone will make them more profitable. In today's market employers endeavor to keep their staffing levels as lean as possible. If they can't clearly see how adding your skills, contacts, and personal qualities will make them more successful, you won't make the cut. It's that simple. You will also be screened out if you cost more than your skills, contacts, and qualities are worth. It doesn't matter if you are a salesperson or an executive, a cleaner, a receptionist, or a warehouse worker.

UNDERSTANDING YOUR IMPACT ON PROFIT

Thinking like an employer means understanding that an employee's impact on profit includes all six areas of PADMAN: Presentation, Ability, Dependability, Motivation, Attitude, and Network. If you have never been involved with the finances of a business, let us give you a quick crash course. Profit is not just money earned. It's the money that's left over after the employers pay *all* their bills, including your paycheck and taxes. If the company makes a million dollars a year and spends $900,000 on bills, they have $100,000 in net profit—this 10 percent is considered good in most industries. But what if they have to pay extra for overtime because employees call in sick, or they have to replace merchandise damaged or stolen by staff, or they become embroiled in expensive lawsuits due to employee actions? Their profit quickly diminishes. And if employees give poor customer service, hurt the company's reputation, or in other ways reduce business, by even just 5 percent, the employers' net profit is reduced by another $50,000! Can you imagine striving all year to build a million-dollar business that earns little or no profit?! This is why hiring wisely is so important to employers. Business owners are in business to make money for themselves or their shareholders—even business owners who care about their employees, love what they do, want to make a difference, and give back to their community. Profit is what keeps them in business, gives you a job, and allows them to do the extra!

➤→ **DID YOU KNOW?**

A full-time employee who takes a fifteen-minute smoking break every two hours costs the company 250 hours each year. That's more than six weeks of time the employer is paying that employee to smoke, not work.

Perhaps you want to go into social work, education, government, or charitable work, and think profitability is not important there. Employers in those work cultures don't use the term "profit," but they still have to keep a close eye on the bottom line. Not-for-profit and government agencies do not have shareholders for whom they must make a profit, but they must still ensure they produce results while staying within budget. If they don't offer a service that donors and taxpayers are willing to support, they won't have the funds to run their program, or the extra "profit" to fund new services, hire new staff, or give raises. Not-for-profits that hire managers who don't produce results within a budget, or employees who can't meet targets and provide a good service without wasting money, are often forced to cut services or go out of business.

Government agencies are a little different because they don't go out of business if they overspend. However, because they rely on public money, overspending can result in higher taxes or a cut in services, both of which create unhappy voters. This is why department heads who don't manage their money wisely are often disciplined or demoted. Whether you want to work in government, not-for-profit, or business, the more clearly you can prove your ability to help employers be profitable, the more valuable you will be.

Seeing the hiring process through the employer's eyes will help you catch and remove the issues that could get you screened out and focus on proving that you will increase profitability. Most people think that job searching is about getting hired. Actually, it's about being the last one standing. Take a look at it from the other side of the desk, and you'll see what we mean.

UNDERSTANDING THE SCREEN-OUT PROCESS

Imagine that a company advertises a single job opening and gets one hundred résumés. The first question the employer asks is, *Who can I get rid of?* He doesn't have time to interview all the candidates, so a computer or junior assistant will quickly skim the résumés for key words and skills, and obvious reasons to put them in the "no" pile, like gaps in work history, little or no experience in the field, and typos or messy appearance. It's a lot like when you skim your email and quickly delete the junk mail so you can focus on the mail that seems worth reading. It's a screen-out process. With thirty to forty résumés remaining in the "maybe" pile, the second question the company asks is, *Who else can I get rid of?* The résumés are reviewed for less obvious screen outs and twenty to thirty more are removed, leaving only eight to twelve in the "maybe" pile. At this point, they have spent less than a minute per résumé (many recruiters brag they'll spend less than ten seconds) and screened out 90 percent of the applicants. Notice that they still don't have a "yes" pile, and the person with the power to hire hasn't yet seen the résumés.

➤ **DID YOU KNOW ? . . .**

You must use the exact terms the employer is looking for. If the computer doesn't see the employer's keywords for the job, you're screened out.

Next, phone calls are made to the remaining eight to twelve candidates to see who's still available, confirm their skills, and begin determining if they'll fit in. If HR or the assistant finds no reason to screen a person out, or if the candidate offers a compelling reason to meet, an initial interview is scheduled. Often, the first interview continues to focus on the question, *Who else can I get rid of?* Only when HR or the assistant has identified the top three to six candidates does the person with the power to hire enter the process and change the question to, *Why should I hire you?* The screen-out process ends, and the hiring process begins, when the decision maker gets involved.

We don't tell you this to depress you, but to point out that if you focus only on your selling points without addressing an employer's concerns, you may be screened out before you get a chance to share those points with the decision maker. We'll show you how to remove your screen outs, as well as prove you'd be great at the job. It all starts with PADMAN. You'll also learn how to skip the screen-out process and go straight to the person with the power to hire, by using side doors. But to do any of this effectively you must understand the employer's perspective.

UNDERSTANDING THE EMPLOYER'S PROBLEM

Employers have limited time and information with which to make an important, expensive hiring decision—that's their problem. They read the résumés, hear the stories, watch the body language, and talk to references, but usually never see the candidate do the job. Often, they will pay out months of salary before knowing whether the person will help create a profit or be an expense that's difficult to unload. This is why they are so picky. They see spelling errors on a résumé and wonder if the person will do sloppy work, isn't very smart, or can't spell. They may decide that a person who shows up four minutes late to the interview is unorganized, has personal problems that will interfere with work, or doesn't value the job. Because employers have this problem, lots of small issues can become the reason you get screened out.

➡ **DID YOU KNOW?**

Many of the side doors we recommend allow employers to see you "do the job," reducing their sense of risk . . . and increases your chance of being hired.

Richard Bolles says in his international bestseller *What Color Is Your Parachute?* "Decisions are based NOT on what is true, but on what is PERCEIVED to be true."[1] We seldom really know what is true. We base our belief on what we experience, see, hear, and take on faith, but when we gain new insights, we adjust what we believe. So an employer's concerns don't even have to be true to get you screened out. What matters is the perception. Take the case of Ralph, a client of ours who was a real flirt. He loved seeing the smile on women's faces when they felt someone thought they were special. He would flirt with store clerks, receptionists, friend's wives, coworkers, even interviewers. No one was safe from his winks and compliments. Ralph was also very happily married and would never take it further than what he called "the feel-good factor." His wife and friends all knew his flirting was harmless and even part of his charm. But to prospective employers, an overtly flirtatious married man could be perceived as a potential messy scandal or lawsuit. Few employers will ask the man how far he plans to take his flirting. They will just assume, and screen accordingly.

You have to think like employers to discover why they are screening you out and find the best way to prove you can help make them profitable. It's not as hard as it sounds if you use PADMAN as your guide. Once you understand the company's needs and concerns in each area of PADMAN, you can highlight the selling points that will impress them and remove the issues that get you screened out. Plus it will help you find the side doors that will get you in front of decision makers. So let's take a look at PADMAN from the employer's perspective.

3

PADMAN: The 6 Reasons You're Hired or Screened Out

PADMAN is all about the employers—their needs, their concerns. Consciously or subconsciously, every interview question you will ever be asked, every reason you will be screened out or hired, and every reason you could get fired or promoted comes from the six areas of PADMAN: Presentation, Ability, Dependability, Motivation, Attitude, and Network.

Each company will define their PADMAN slightly differently, because each company has a different image, personality, and set of goals. Understanding how employers judge each category allows you to identify their preferences and tailor your marketing strategy. For example, if the company prides itself on an *attitude* of great customer service, then your marketing materials should highlight positive results or comments from past customers. If part of their *motivation* is "giving back to the community" and you're also community-minded, add a Community and

Company Projects section to your résumé where you list the organizations or projects you've participated in (on your own or with previous companies) and what you accomplished—just be sure you don't list groups that could be controversial. Adding unique sections might be unusual, but to get noticed you must stand out for reasons the employer values. If the company presents itself as fast-paced and cutting-edge, mirror that in your approach by being concise and to the point, and perhaps use a speculative letter with a link to a video résumé. Your goal is to present yourself as their ideal candidate while deliberately minimizing issues that might get you screened out along the way.

To succeed, you may need to adjust how you talk, dress, or act during your job search and at work so that you match what is expected in the new company culture. We call this becoming *bicultural*—that is, having the ability to succeed in two different cultures. People who immigrate to our country and want to succeed in this business culture are acutely aware of this concept. But it applies to all of us. Often our social or home culture follows different rules from the business we are trying to enter. A simple example is that it's not uncommon to yell up the stairs when talking to a family member, but in most business cultures yelling across a room is considered very unprofessional. The rules of one culture are not superior to the other. Different behavior is simply appropriate in different settings. So as you investigate your prospective

---

➤ **DID YOU KNOW?**

Employers are often more lax with lower paid employees when it comes to matching their company culture and more exacting as you move up the company ladder. To be perceived as promotable, even before you're hired, reflect more closely the company's PADMAN.

---

employer's PADMAN, determine what adjustments you will need to make while at work to get hired, retained, and promoted.

As you read about what employers are looking for in each area of PADMAN, think about past employers and identify their PADMAN. This exercise will help you understand what to look for in future employers. Researching your prospective employer's PADMAN takes time—but investing a few hours or days now will help you avoid months of unsuccessful job searching.

REASON 1: PRESENTATION

From the employer's perspective, presentation is not just a matter of looking good; it's about looking, sounding, and acting like the employer. Each company has its own image; it's part of their marketing strategy. They want every employee to positively represent the company to the public and coworkers. So, when hiring, they scrutinize everything from your clothing and hairstyle to your handshake and hygiene, from your accent and grammar to your eye contact and body language, and from the type of work you've done in the past to the image it projects. For some jobs, even things that seem like minor issues can be important, such as the car you drive, your table manners, or your golf handicap.

We've all heard the old saying "You only get one chance to make a great first impression." Although it's true, in the job search it's not just the first impression in the interview that counts. Throughout the hiring process, lots of people are watching you. The clerk or receptionist who accepts your application or résumé often has the power to screen you out, and even if you shine in the interview, if you don't continue to impress the employer in your follow-up, you could lose the offer. Poor presentation can get you screened out, just as the right presentation can persuade employers to overlook weaknesses in other areas.

You may already know a lot about making the right presentation, but there's more. When companies are hiring, consciously or subconsciously, they look for the answers to their key question for each area of PADMAN. The question lurking in their minds about your presentation is, *Do you look, sound, and act in a way that positively represents my company?*

Think of the difference in image, speech, and mannerisms between successful salespeople at an upscale jewelry boutique and a skateboard shop. If you switched them, the customers of both would respond negatively. Presentation matters. It's about the way you look, but also how you behave and what you sound like. The first impression customers have of a company is usually made by employees. Imagine your first impression of a company whose delivery driver wore a stained, wrinkled, smelly uniform or whose account rep sent emails full of typos and poor grammar. We make assumptions about a company based on who they hire. For better or worse, every employee represents the entire company. Even if the job you want has no customer contact, presentation still matters because it sends a message about what is acceptable to other employees, potential employees, vendors, and anyone who knows where you work.

Good presentation is important, but having the *right* presentation matters most of all. Employers know that a strong company image helps establish a strong company reputation and culture. What they look for when judging presentation depends on the message the company is trying to send about who they are. Of course presentation includes appearance, manners, and how you speak and write, but also anything that customers or the team think is important, like the quality of your tools, brand of clothing, use of slang, and more. Increasingly it incorporates anything available for public scrutiny, such as your online persona and your behavior when driving a company vehicle or attending public functions. Presentation can also include issues that are not supposed to be considered, like your age, race, gender, weight, sexuality, disability, pregnancy, and obvious lifestyle values. Ignoring this fact doesn't make it go away, it just leaves you unprepared.

There are three ways to convince employers you match their company image. The easiest is to target companies with images similar to your own. Consider businesses where you are a customer and places where people like you already work. A second option is to adjust your presentation so you will easily fit into a company's image. The third option is to persuade the employer that your image, which is different than the company's, won't be a problem. The third option isn't the easiest, but it can be done. In Part 2, we'll show you how to do all three. Whatever image you present in the interview must be maintained the entire time you work for the company, or until you've earned permission to adjust it. If you won't be happy doing this, consider a company that matches your current image better.

Here are some tips for addressing common employer complaints and mistakes in interviews:

- Turn off your mobile phone or iPod.
- Don't chew gum or suck on breath mints.
- Don't accept an offer of coffee or water, because it's a distraction, and accidents can happen.
- Don't smell of alcohol or cigarettes, or be under the influence of drugs.
- Don't interrupt or contradict the interviewer, or try to make yourself look smarter by making her look dumb or wrong.

- Don't swear, even if the employer does.
- Avoid blowing your nose in front of the interviewer; instead wipe it discreetly. If you are truly sick, reschedule.
- Avoid sweaty palms by applying antiperspirant to your palms several hours before.
- Avoid profuse sweating by adhering panty shields inside the underarms of your shirt and arriving early enough to discreetly dispose of them in the restroom before meeting the employer—it's a little unusual, but it works.
- Smile, make eye contact with each person, and greet them as you enter.
- Wait to be told where to sit.
- Watch your body language. Leaning back in your chair is often interpreted as disinterest or arrogance, while leaning forward shows interest and involvement.
- Avoid fidgeting—cross your ankles and loosely fold your hands in your lap. The more prepared you are, the more relaxed you will be.
- Show your professionalism, promotability, and respect for the company by dressing one notch better than you would once you were working. For example, a software engineer should wear slacks, a button-up shirt, and a sports jacket, even though these guys are notorious for their "comfortable" attire on the job. A cargo loader should wear new jeans, a T-shirt underneath an ironed, button-down shirt, and clean, polished work boots; if he showed up in a suit, many employers would assume he belonged in the office, not on the dock. There are a few exceptions to this rule. If you are young, dress more than one notch up, to show respect, maturity, and most important, a willingness to adjust in order to

please the employer—you get extra points for effort. If you might be considered overqualified, minimize the perception that you are above the position by dressing just as you would on the job.

- Always thank the interviewer for his time.

➤ **DID YOU KNOW?**

In some cultures, using a superior's first name is considered disrespectful or unprofessional, but in the West, it shows friendliness and approachability. Westerners value *professional informality*, demonstrated by casual dress Friday, using bullet points rather than full sentences, talking in a familiar manner to all types of people, and using first names rather than titles or last names once you know people. In general, only older, senior businesspeople continue to use their last name after the initial meeting, but even this is changing.

Let's follow Amanda as she prepares her presentation for an interview as a graphic designer with an independent publisher of spiritual and self-help books. The advertisement and job description tell very little about the company image, so a few days before the interview Amanda browses the company website and visits the office before a lunch meeting with a friend who works in the Accounting Department. She notices that people are dressed smart-casual and that the environment feels relaxed. Later, Amanda reflects that her interest in personal and spiritual growth will give her a lot to talk about in the interview, but her style may be too slick and high-powered. She decides to wear nice slacks and a casual jacket, rather than a tailored suit. She also organizes her portfolio to highlight work that is similar to projects the company would ask her to do.

You may think Amanda is very lucky to have a friend who can

give her insider information. It wasn't luck, it was part of her plan, and it's a great way for you to get a job, too. Amanda started her job search by listing everyone she knew who had a strong network or worked for companies that might need her talent. She reached out to each of her acquaintances, pitched herself, and asked them to help her connect with employers. Throughout her job search, Amanda talked with friends and colleagues to discover opportunities, and wasn't shy about asking for introductions and information. There is a good chance that you already know someone who knows someone who needs your talent. If Amanda hadn't known someone who worked at this company, she still could have visited the publisher's office to request information as a prospective customer, client, investor, or even researcher for an article or term paper (if she was a student). Or she could simple explain that she had heard great things about the company and wanted to learn a bit more before offering her résumé. Perhaps she would have made friends with the receptionist or staff person she spoke with and received insider information. You will meet Amanda again as we explore each area of PADMAN. She'll illustrate how to use some of our ideas and techniques to create a more effective job search.

REASON 2: ABILITY

Job seekers often think ability is the most important of the six PADMAN areas. In reality, lack of ability may get you screened out, but it's usually one of the other five areas that get you hired. All the top candidates will have the ability to do the job, so the deciding factor becomes who the employer likes best and believes customers and employees will like, who he can depend on to work in the company's best interest or achieve their goals, or who has access to a network they need. Only in the case of technical jobs for which there are few people with the required skills is ability the final reason you are hired. In fact, we often hear employers say, "If someone has the right attitude and some raw talent, I can teach them the skills."

> *From the employer's perspective*, ability is not just the skills you have gained from formal work experience, education, and training—it's how well you can apply them. Lack of proven ability is one of the first factors used to screen applicants out. If you have proven your ability in most areas the employer needs, then your unpaid work, raw talent, aptitude, and life learning can make up for the rest. In today's fast-changing world, employers also look beyond current knowledge and experience, for the highly valued ability to learn and adapt.

When employers are considering hiring you, their question about your ability is, *Can you do the job, or learn it quickly?* Ability is about getting results in a reasonable time frame. To decide if you can produce results, employers look at your work history, education, licenses, and certifications. You might be surprised to discover that higher education is valued differently in the U.S. business culture than in many others. Many American entrepreneurs were CEOs of million-dollar companies before getting an advanced degree, or any degree. The top value in American business, particularly small to midsize companies, is producing results quickly. An advanced degree doesn't prove you can produce results, so don't assume your education will get you a job. It's merely a selling point. Education is valued more by corporate America, where universities are seen as places to learn to follow instructions, assimilate and disseminate information, complete tasks even if you have to stay up all night, be exposed to important ideas, and build a valuable professional network . . . but they also want proof you can produce results.

Proof of results can also be drawn from military service, natural talents, hobbies, parenting, volunteer or civic responsibilities, and life skills. Proof can even be gained from unexpected experiences like mandated community service or a government program, prison, or a drug treatment program. If you are changing fields or returning to the workforce, use transferable skills from all parts of your life to prove you have the ability to produce the results the employer needs. We show you how in Chapter 9.

Job advertisements, postings, and descriptions generally list what employers are looking for in terms of ability, so this is easy to discover. But employers seldom expect you to know every aspect of a new job. They understand that there is always a learning curve, even if it simply means learning how to do it their way. Employers do, however, expect you to demonstrate commitment to the job by having gained the core qualifications and possessing the raw talent to quickly learn what you don't know. Many employers are willing to teach some vocational skills if you match most of their needs in the other five areas of PADMAN. If you are young, they may even be willing to help develop your presentation. Few employers feel equipped or responsible to teach attitude, dependability, or motivation. These are basic qualities you must prove you already have.

Throughout the job search, actively demonstrate the skills you say you have, because the employer will be watching. If you say you're great at managing projects but in the interview it's clear you didn't bother to research the company, bring information the employer may request, or prepare good answers, the employer will assume you are not. This can even cause her to question whether the other skills you've touted meet the company's standards.

Watch how Amanda continues to prepare for her interview as

a graphic designer for an independent publisher. A review of the job description convinces her she can easily show that she has the required design skills, education, and experience. She knows all the software packages they use, and can demonstrate her ability to draw freehand and on a computer. She's also confident she can quickly learn their project management system. Amanda's one concern is that the company uses Mac computers and she uses a PC. She immediately appeals to a fellow designer who uses a Mac to give her a crash course, and talks him into letting her borrow several books so she can study up. She also registers for a Mac class offered the Saturday after the interview. Lastly, she prepares a good answer to explain her plan to quickly increase her proficiency with a Mac and purchase a Mac laptop if she gets the job.

Notice how Amanda continues to tap into her network to overcome the issues that could get her screened out. It's important to mobilize every resource you have. Think of yourself as a consultant; it's up to you to make it happen. Amanda isn't lucky, she's smart and serious about getting the job.

REASON 3: DEPENDABILITY

From the employer's perspective, dependability is not just about showing up on time every day. In fact, most employers don't want you to show up at all if you are just there for a paycheck, constantly watch the clock, are emotionally unstable, do minimal or poor-quality work, steal, speak negatively about the company, or in other ways fail to work in *their* best interest. They are putting their reputation and profitability in your hands, so they must sense that you are reliable and trustworthy, even when no one is watching.

When you think "dependability," you probably think of coming to work each day on time. In Western business culture, on time means arriving five to fifteen minutes before an interview or meeting. Showing up too early is seen as unprofessional or inconvenient because someone must entertain you. Arriving late is viewed as undervaluing the person or the meeting. This may be different from your social culture. Many Latin American cultures perceive being late as a distinction of those who are important. Many Asian cultures consider it the height of rudeness to end an interaction just because you have another appointment. In Western business culture, companies want employees who show up every day on time, but dependability runs deeper than timekeeping.

The question employers are asking themselves is, *Will you work in my company's best interest?* They need to know they can trust you with their money, customers, secrets, products, and reputation. Few employers will hire even an entry-level worker who might steal from them or a customer, lie to get what he wants (even on their application), or let it slip that he wouldn't be caught dead using the company's product or service. Employers want people they can depend on to follow instructions, produce the quality and quantity of work required, meet deadlines, and stay until the job is done.

➤ **DID YOU KNOW?**

Most jobs require multitasking—working on several tasks at once with an understanding of which is most important. When you complete one task, you are already working on others, with little time for celebration or reflection. If you have a one-thing-at-a-time approach, it often causes employers to doubt your capacity to get results and meet deadlines.

Dependability also includes *loyalty*, a big concept that can be seen in small things, like how long you plan to stay or whether you talk up or bad-mouth former companies—so don't speak negatively about past employers, or the interviewer may assume she's next.

To assess dependability, employers look at your work history and education, but also consider things you might not think of, like emotional stability, lawsuits, illness, childcare, health and safety, and ability to leave personal problems at home. Employers only discover these types of problems if you tell them, or one of your references does, or you demonstrate the problem during the hiring process. Since dependability is such a broad category, and incorporates concerns that are not always fair or legal, you must think like a picky employer to see them, and then use the techniques we teach you in later chapters to prove you'll work in the employer's best interest.

Amanda needs to prove she is dependable so she can land the job as a graphic designer for an independent publisher of self-help and spiritual books. Over the years, as a freelance designer, she has cultivated a strong reputation for looking out for her customer's interest and getting jobs done on time. Amanda has several customers who are happy to act as references. When she calls HR to learn more about the job and why it is currently available, she learns that the company is growing, and wants to hire an in-house designer because it's more cost-effective than using freelancers. She decides to play up the fact that she offers the flexibility and speed of a freelancer, and the low cost and reliability of a full-time employee.

Thinking from the employer's perspective, Amanda identifies two possible concerns the employer might have about her dependability: She is the mother of a young child and has a ninety-minute round-trip commute. In case the issues arise, Amanda prepares to explain her child care plan and her husband's ability to help, and how she looks forward to using the commute to listen to audio books and replenish herself spiritually. She would like to work from home several days a week and realizes it might be possible in the future, but decides not to mention it until after she is hired and has proven the employer can trust her talent and work ethic. Her willingness to take work home to insure projects get done on time will help her build a case for working from home later. Now let's assess your strengths and weaknesses in the next area of PADMAN and see how Amanda addresses hers.

REASON 4: MOTIVATION

From the employers' perspective, motivation is not just about taking initiative, doing the extra or being ambitious—it's about using all that to help them achieve *their* goals. Proving you are motivated begins not with taking action, but with researching the company's goals. If your actions move the company down a path it doesn't want to go, you are seen as a loose cannon dangerously shooting off in the wrong direction. Companies are looking for employees who understand that their job is not just a list of tasks in a job description, but rather helping the company be profitable and achieve its mission—regardless of the employee's job title.

Most of us think we know what a "motivated" person looks like. However, this is the area in which the employers' mind-set is *most* different from yours, so watch out. Many job seekers miss the mark in this area, so if you hit it, you can outshine your competition and get offers quicker. The question employers ask regarding your motivation is, *Do your actions and goals promote my company and its goals?* Who would you hire as a youth worker: the person who believes "better safe than sorry" or the one who believes "childhood comes with a few skinned knees"? It depends on your company goals. If the goal is to teach kids to take risks and be self-sufficient, then the youth worker who is always babying the kids would be the loose cannon. As an employee, your initiative *only counts if it helps the company achieve its goals.* Notice that we didn't say *your* goals, or the goals *you* think the company should have, or the goals you *wish* they had. From the employers' perspective, you are motivated when your energy is directed toward achieving *the company's* goals. So begin by researching them.

To discover the company goals, review their website and mission statement, talk with staff and customers, and search the Internet. However, the company's goals are not the only goals you want to discover; after all it's the manager who makes the final hiring decision. Whether you like it or not, managers tend to hire people they believe will help them succeed, who share their professional and personal goals and will make them look good. Reflect on your work life and you'll probably find cases where an employee was hired or prized by a manager for those reasons. To discover a manager's goals, talk with friends or associates who

---

➡ DID YOU KNOW?

It's perfectly acceptable to contact HR or a friendly insider before your interview to learn more about the employers' PADMAN. Get clarifying details about the abilities they are looking for, how long the position has been open, and why. Ask about the company's image, personality, mission, target customers, and department structure. You can even inquire about the manager's goals and preferences, and be sure to thank the person for his time. Stick to the positive, and make sure your tone, questions, and background noise make a positive impression.

---

work for the company, review the manager's bio on the company website and his LinkedIn profile, follow him on Twitter if possible. Look the manager up online and read any website contributions, blogs, or articles written by or about her. If your first interview is not with your potential manager, but with HR or someone focused on screening out, include a few questions about the manager: *If I get the position, who will I be working under? What do you believe are their most important priorities for the job? I know teamwork is important. What can you tell me about this person's management style?*

Finally, use what you have learned to show your motivation. Interviewers often ask what you know about the company and why you want to work for them. Every company believes they are unique, even if they offer the same service or product as another company down the road. Make them feel special and chosen by demonstrating that you know what's important to them. Highlight the qualities, attitudes, and skills they value most—in your key message, résumé, cover letter, speculative letter, good answers, side door selection—in all aspects of your job search. Few job seekers take the time to research or demonstrate that they care about these goals, so it's a great opportunity to stand out from the crowd.

Walk with Amanda as she prepares to prove her motivation in her interview. On the company's website, she discovers that their mission is "to promote the spiritual and emotional health of readers by producing meaningful, beautiful works." The job advertisement states that they value customer loyalty, have very low staff turnover, and pride themselves on being a "family." So Amanda calls her friend who works for the publisher and told her about the job, to ask how the company mission plays out in daily operations. Amanda learns that the company wants customers to see them as approachable, open-minded, and positive, but very professional and efficient. Amanda memorizes the company's one-line mission statement and thinks of specific ways she can promote it as a graphic designer. She also prepares several stories that show she is open-minded, professional, and can help create loyal customers. In the interview and in her follow-up, she plans to behave in a way that proves she is both efficient and approachable. Finally, she prepares to share the reasons she wants to be part of the company "family" and some details of her own spiritual journey, in case the subject arises.

REASON 5: ATTITUDE

From the employer's perspective, attitude is not just about being friendly and respectful; it's about fitting in. One employer may love that you are happy and talkative, while it drives another crazy. Your personality needs to fit with the company's culture, whether it's trendy, sophisticated, down-home, socially responsible, fun, creative, green, high-powered, or something else. Employers need to believe that their customers and team will respond positively to you. They must also know that your work attitude matches the specific job, whether you're flexible or structured, eager to learn or happy to do repetitive tasks, safety-conscious or risk-taking, fast-paced or laid-back . . . You get the idea.

Having a "good attitude" is about reflecting the company's personality. The key questions employers ask themselves about your attitude are, *Do I want to work with you?* and *Will you fit into my company culture?* So ask yourself if you are someone the employers' customers will be drawn to. Will the interviewer and her team want to work with you for twenty, forty, or sixty hours a week? If your job is outside a team, do you have the personality required to get it done on your own?

Employers are drawn to people who project their company personality in a positive, confident way, but hearing no or nothing at all when you are job searching can quickly have a negative effect on your attitude. Fear can show through. During the interview, employers often ask tough questions or create a stressful environment, just to watch your attitude as you handle it. In these situations, fear can grow, and if it looks like anger, desperation, or depression, most employers will cut their losses and screen you out early. On the other hand, if you anticipate the stressful environment and come prepared, your attitude will remain positive, confident, and respectful, which often makes the employer willing to overlook weaknesses in other areas. Employers repeatedly tell us that if a person has the right attitude, they can teach the skills.

Attitude is as much about your outlook on work as it is about your personality. Different employers value different attitudes, but there are some that all employers value. At the top of most lists are a positive confidence (we talk more about it in Chapter 14), a strong work ethic that compels you to always do your best, and a willingness to do the extra and stay until the job is done. Staff who want to be well regarded or advance generally give an extra two to five hours a week. Managers are typically expected to work five to ten extra hours a week, and senior managers often work twenty-plus extra hours weekly by coming early, staying late, working through lunch, taking work home, or working weekends. If you are unwilling to do the extra, you may be seen as lacking commitment. When employers consider who to lay off or promote, who do you think they select? Other highly valued attitudes include flexibility and an ability to cope with change; a genuine interest in the work, industry, or company; an ability to get along well with others and show respect; a willingness to do what's asked even if it's "not your job"; and a commitment to continuous improvement.

DID YOU KNOW?

Employers often evaluate your interest in a field by what you do or learn on your own time. Your interest in the company is usually determined by your knowledge about it and willingness to do the extra.

Staff attitudes affect every aspect of a company, including teamwork, productivity, recruitment of new staff, job satisfaction, sales, word-of-mouth marketing, and repeat business. This is why most employers, when asked to prioritize the PADMAN areas, rank attitude as number one or number two. The easiest way to get a yes to the questions, *Do I want to work with you?* and *Will you fit into my company culture?* is to target jobs and company cultures that fit your personality. Another option, if your personality isn't a natural fit, is to temper your attitude so it promotes the company culture. If you do this and get the job, then in order to keep it, you must maintain the tempered attitude every minute you are working or representing the employer.

Now let's see how Amanda discovers and proves she has the attitude needed as a graphic designer for the publisher she is interviewing with. When she visits her friend who works for the publisher, she asks for a quick tour of the offices to get a sense of the culture. Personality-wise, she feels like she is a fit. However, for the last four years Amanda has been her own boss working on freelance projects. Clearly, she has a passion for bringing a customer's vision to life, but in this job, she would work for a creative designer on a team and not directly with customers. She realizes the employer may wonder if she is overqualified, can work under someone else's leadership, and is willing to be part of a team. She plans to share a few stories that portray her as a team player who can take instruction and do things "their way," and prepares a good answer that explains why she is choosing not to work for herself or become a creative director. Like Amanda, find ways to demonstrate that your attitude fits with both the company culture and the job.

REASON 6: NETWORK

From the employer's perspective, network is *not* just about who you know. It's about having access to the right people, and not attracting the wrong ones. To determine your network, employers consider your professional and personal contacts. This includes people you went to school with, past coworkers, industry contacts, and anyone listed as a reference. It also includes friends, family, acquaintances, neighbors, and social networking sites you've joined, as well as associations, clubs, and other groups you are or have been a part of. Employers want to know whether the people in your network will benefit their company as customers, investors, and business allies, or if they could hurt the company by creating concern among staff, customers, or the public.

When a company hires you, they get your network, too, and whatever reputation comes with it. Having worked in prestigious jobs or companies can be a plus, but employers may also be concerned to learn if you've been employed in a questionable job or company. Also, they consider your personal network, which is often underappreciated by job seekers. We know that the right connections can help us land the job, but we forget that the wrong connections can lose us a job. Your network is not just your past coworkers and the references you give employers. It also takes in your social networks, including online, and anyone the employer associates with you during the hiring process. When companies are hiring, their question about your network is, "Do the people you know and attract benefit my company, or could they cause concern?"

Many employers will look at your online "friends." An ExecuNet survey about reputation management found that 86 percent of executive recruiters look online for information that goes beyond a candidate's résumé, and nearly seven in ten say job candidates prospects improve when positive information is found online.[1] So create an online image in the same way you craft your image for the interview. Start by separating your personal and professional lives online. Most social networking sites allow you to control who has access to your information. If employers try to connect with you on a site that contains details that could distract them from hiring you, decline to connect. Then, send a quick email acknowledging their request, letting them know that you reserve the site for personal and family interactions, and redirecting them to your public site. View any public social networking site you use as a job search site, and create an online identity that shows potential employers how you benefit them. Choose a screen name that highlights a quality, skill, or area of interest you want employers to know about, or simply use your formal name. Craft your profile to clearly communicate your talents and selling points. Make sure each posting and every group you join promotes you to employers. Your photo should be a headshot with a pleasant expression, or a graphic that markets you. LinkedIn, Facebook, and Twitter are free to join, easy-to-use, and can connect you to many people very quickly.

The importance of your network depends on who you know and the job you want. In some cases, your network is even more important than your experience. For example, an employer might hire a salesperson who has no experience but has a natural sales ability, a huge local network among potential customers, and is respected by everyone in town, before he would hire a salesperson with ten years' experience who is new to the area and has no local contacts. The experienced candidate could take months to generate income, while the well-networked candidate could deliver immediately if she uses her contacts to set up meetings at which the employer trains her on-the-job.

➤ **DID YOU KNOW?**

Your network is not just important if you work in sales. A positive network is important in lots of jobs—event planning, fundraising, construction, procurement, social work, small business, public relations, most management jobs—and a negative network is detrimental in most jobs.

A positive network can get your foot in the door for most jobs. Do you know people who could become customers, or generate customers, for the employers you want to work for? Do you know experts in the field who lend credibility or would share their expertise? Do you have contacts who can help the company grow, run smoother, or function more cost-effectively? This is what employers are looking for, so use these valuable connections in your job search and make employers aware of them. Also remember that negative connections can get you screened out, so before you begin interacting with employers decide what you want them to know about your network. For example, if someone accompanies you to submit an application or résumé, be sure that person highlights the image or attitudes you want to project, rather than possible barriers, such as child care needs, or friends the employer wouldn't want hanging around. Employers probably won't bring up these issues, so it's your responsibility to insure that your network doesn't cause concern.

Let's see how Amanda deals with the network question as she prepares for her interview. Amanda looks for connections she has in common with the company, or whom they might want to know. She has a friend who works in their Accounting Department who has a great reputation and has been with them for years, so Amanda plans to mention their friendship in the interview. Amanda has several well-respected associates, has worked for a few prestigious customers, and attended a renowned school of design, so she prepares a list of references for the interviewer. Plus, if the opportunity arises, she'll mention that she has a great source for discounted software. Finally, Amanda wisely decides not to mention the Mac designer who helped her prepare for the interview, because he had a falling out with the company's creative director and refers to the company as a bunch of "spiritual freaks."

Amanda started her job search by targeting several companies where she had a positive connection, then invested a couple of days researching and proving she could meet each company's needs, planning her responses, and removing her barriers. You saw how she did it for one independent publisher. A few days' effort up front saved her months of frustrating, unsuccessful job searching.

To prove to employers that you can increase their profit, follow Amanda's example. Research your answers to these six questions before the interview. Clarify your "soon-to-be" employer's top needs in each area of PADMAN. Don't just focus on ability, because most people who get past the initial screen out are perceived as able to do or to learn the job. Remember, the more senior the position and the closer you get to the short list (the top three to six candidates), the pickier employers will be about what they need and what they screen out for. The one who is hired is the one who stands out in all six areas.

4

It Takes More Than Ability
to Get Hired

Employers are looking for wise investments—and employees are often their largest investment. That's why they compare you against their PADMAN for the job. All six areas are important, but each employer prioritizes them differently depending on the job and the company goals. When hiring for customer service jobs, employers often rate presentation and attitude at the top. If the job requires discretion or one person to complete tasks before another can start, then dependability is number one. Employers in fast-growing or quickly changing companies often value motivation most. Those hiring for scientific and highly technical jobs generally care most about ability, and those looking for people to do sales or resource development often rank network as paramount. If you are very strong in the two or three areas an employer needs most, he may overlook or work with your weaknesses. However, if you are weak in an area an employer values, you'll need to fix it to get hired. For example, if an employer is hiring front office staff and a candidate hasn't updated her image in more than fifteen years, the employer may worry that the person has outdated skills, resists change, or won't impress customers or other staff. This doesn't mean the candidate can't do the job, but it makes the employer wonder if what he will gain outweighs the risks. The key is to ensure that your overall value in PADMAN outweighs any risks the employer takes in hiring you.

Another thing to consider is that ads and job descriptions tend to focus on ability, but employers want more than what they ask for. Think about it. Few employers ask for people who use manners, speak business English, work safely, and are easy to get along with, but most employers want these things. You must look beyond what they ask for, and address their spoken and unspoken needs. Your PADMAN doesn't have to be perfect, but it does have to be fixable. We'll show you how.

MAKING PADMAN WORK FOR YOU

Albert Einstein said that "doing the same thing over and over again and expecting different results is insanity." New information and techniques are only helpful if you do something new with them! We designed the PADMAN Plan to help you identify what you can do differently to get hired. It's a simple way to create a tailored marketing plan for each job you want. It helps you identify what an employer wants, then maximize your proof so the employer quickly sees that you meet his needs. It also helps you identify and overcome all the barriers standing in your way. Barriers are any issues that cause the employer to screen you out. They are not always fair, true, politically correct, or even legal, but each can be overcome using the six solution tools we'll teach you in Part 3.

Download the PADMAN Plan worksheet under "Free Tools" at www.the6reasons.com, or create your own in a notebook using the sample in the appendix, then follow these five steps: (1) choose your target; (2) list the employer's needs; (3) prove you can do the job; (4) identify your barriers; and (5) create your solutions.

Step 1: Choose Your Job Target

Start by identifying the job you want and writing it at the top of your PADMAN Plan as shown in the example on page 51. Include both the position and field (that is, receptionist in construction, physical therapist for a sports team). A specific job target is important because the employers' needs and the reasons they screen out may be different for each job. And it helps you focus only on the proof and barriers relevant to the job you want. Any accomplishments or barriers unrelated to your job target are nonissues and shouldn't be included. If you're unsure which jobs you would enjoy and do well, read Chapter 13. If you need more help, read *What Color Is Your Parachute?* by Richard Bolles. It has helped millions of people determine the right career for them.

Step 2: List the Employer's Needs

Once you've clarified your target, identify your prospective employer's needs for that job and list them on your Plan. Proving you can meet those needs is why you'll get hired, and failing to meet them is why you'll get screened out! Remember, employers care about all six areas of PADMAN, so look for their top three to six needs in each area. And be specific—for example, "computer skills" becomes "knowledge of Microsoft Professional Office Suite, with ability to create Excel spreadsheets." Here are a few tips for discovering employers' top needs:

Look at what they ask for in each area of PADMAN. Review the job posting and job description, and visit http://online .onetcenter.org for a list of common requirements (type the title in the "Occupational Quick Search" box and select your job from the list of related titles).

Learn as much as you can about the company. Search the company website and for articles about it, and visit and talk to current employees, customers, and associates. Learn what's important to the company, what makes it unique, what it is most proud of, what's new, and what's changing. Remember, employers will only add to their payroll costs if they believe you will help them solve a problem, meet a need, or make money.

Talk with people outside the company who hire, train, or supervise others doing the same job. Ask what makes an employee great in this position. Talk with employment specialists, recruiters, headhunters, résumé writers, and staffing professionals who work in the field, to discover what employers value most in the job. If you don't know anyone personally, make cold calls. When calling, introduce yourself as someone considering a career change (or depending on your situation, a blogger researching an article, a student writing a thesis or investigating the industry, or a qualified candidate considering relocation)—but not a job seeker. If they think you want a job, they'll say they're not hiring and end the conversation. Be clear that you just want information. Here's a sample script for career changers:

> *Hi, this is Jane Doe. I'm hoping you can help me with some information. I'm considering a career change and want to*

learn more about your industry before I decide whether to make the move. May I ask you three quick questions?

They are busy, so let them know you'll keep it short.

I have (list your top three transferable skills). Do I meet the needs for an XYZ position? . . . Great! I know excelling requires more than just skills. What do you think are the most important qualities for the job? . . . And lastly, to make sure I'd be a good match, are there qualities or attitudes that can cause a problem in that position; maybe things that get in the way of someone being great at it? . . . Thank you for your time.

Adjust it to suit your style, the person you are talking to, or specific information you want to gain, such as *Do you know of instances where someone who doesn't have an ABC certificate has been hired?*

Discover the industry's current priorities. What are the new problems they face, and opportunities they hope to take advantage of? What new technologies and solutions exist? Read industry magazines, blogs, newsletters, and articles. Attend industry events. Talk with industry insiders and past business associates.

Continue your research during the interview. Listen closely to the questions asked, because they indicate what is important to the employer. For example:

- *How many years of experience do you have?* and *Do you have an ABC certificate?* reveal the vocational skills the employer thinks ensure your ability to make the company profitable.
- *How would you deal with customers in XYZ situation?* and *We invest a lot of training in our staff, so what*

would you like to be doing in five years? offer insight into how the employer prioritizes PADMAN. If he's had difficulty finding people with these qualities, he'll probably ask follow-up questions.

- *What does being "dependable" mean to you?* and *Have you ever been fired or committed a crime?* highlight past problems the employer wants to know will not be a problem with you.
- *Why did you leave your last job?* and *Why would your past coworkers say we should hire you?* are designed to assess your attitudes and whether you'll fit with the employer's customers and coworkers.

Once you learn from the first interview what is specifically important to that employer, use it to tailor your responses and prepare for the next round of interviews.

As you discover your employer's needs, list them on your Plan, next to the corresponding PADMAN area. Don't be afraid to list needs you can't meet, because we'll show you how to overcome those obstacles. Remember, not listing a need doesn't make it go away, it just makes you unprepared. Also, list additional selling points you have that the employer may want for this job but didn't ask for, such as a great memory for faces and names, or as in our example on page 51, a strong connections with local trainers and kennels or referrals. Your next step will be to develop persuasive selling points for each.

If the thought of doing this for every employer you're going to send a résumé to feels overwhelming, then don't. Instead, select one industry and job title and create a general PADMAN Plan and résumé for it. Next, select three companies you want to work for within that industry and research their specific PADMAN as Amanda did. Then tailor your key message, cover letter, and

SAMPLE PADMAN PLAN

	1. Job Target Office Assistant in a veterinary office	
	2. Employer Needs	**3. My Proof** Facts, Story, Demonstration, Credible Reference
P Presentation	• Casual professional image	☐ Facts ☐ Story ☐ Demo ☐ CR _____
	• Good phone voice	☐ Facts ☐ Story ☐ Demo ☐ CR _____
	• Good handwriting	☐ Facts ☐ Story ☐ Demo ☐ CR _____
	• Energetic demeanor	☐ Facts ☐ Story ☐ Demo ☐ CR _____
A Ability	• Proficient in MS Suite	☐ Facts ☐ Story ☐ Demo ☐ CR _____
	• Know vet terms	☐ Facts ☐ Story ☐ Demo ☐ CR _____
	• Good with animals	☐ Facts ☐ Story ☐ Demo ☐ CR _____
	• Customer service exp	☐ Facts ☐ Story ☐ Demo ☐ CR _____
D Dependability	• At work daily by 7:45 a.m.	☐ Facts ☐ Story ☐ Demo ☐ CR _____
	• Organized so paperwork is accessible	☐ Facts ☐ Story ☐ Demo ☐ CR _____
	• Complete tasks on time	☐ Facts ☐ Story ☐ Demo ☐ CR _____
	• Honest/reliable with handling money	☐ Facts ☐ Story ☐ Demo ☐ CR _____
M Motivation	• Task completer	☐ Facts ☐ Story ☐ Demo ☐ CR _____
	• Loves animals but can handle seeing them put down	☐ Facts ☐ Story ☐ Demo ☐ CR _____
	• Good team player	☐ Facts ☐ Story ☐ Demo ☐ CR _____
	• Willing to do menial tasks	☐ Facts ☐ Story ☐ Demo ☐ CR _____
A Attitude	• Compassionate	☐ Facts ☐ Story ☐ Demo ☐ CR _____
	• Emotionally strong	☐ Facts ☐ Story ☐ Demo ☐ CR _____
	• Friendly	☐ Facts ☐ Story ☐ Demo ☐ CR _____
	• Willing to learn	☐ Facts ☐ Story ☐ Demo ☐ CR _____
N Network	• Connections with local pet stores, trainers, and kennels	☐ Facts ☐ Story ☐ Demo ☐ CR _____
	• ASPCA volunteer	☐ Facts ☐ Story ☐ Demo ☐ CR _____
	•	☐ Facts ☐ Story ☐ Demo ☐ CR _____
	•	☐ Facts ☐ Story ☐ Demo ☐ CR _____

spontaneous letters specifically for them. Lastly, determine the best side doors to use (we'll show you how to do all of this in the chapters ahead). We guarantee it will consume less time than submitting hundreds of applications or résumés over the next several months, and will produce better results. Plus, it will increase your confidence and prepare you to stand out in the interview so you get the job. If you are interested in a couple of different industries or job titles, you can follow the same process for each.

PART

2

How to Prove You Are the Best Candidate

Being good at a job is not enough to get hired. Have you ever applied for a job that was given to someone else and thought, *I'm better at that job than she is*? If you're better, why did the employer hire the other person instead of you? Most likely, she proved she offered something the employer needed that you did not offer. We're not saying that you didn't have what the employer needed. We're saying you didn't *prove it*.

Every day, thousands of great applicants are screened out because, although they might be great for the job, they didn't prove it. Employers are not mind readers. If you don't offer clear evidence, they will go with the person who does. And remember, employers care about all six areas of PADMAN, not just ability. In addition to skills, the best candidate will also have the right *presentation* and *attitude*, be *dependable*, with a *motivation* to help the company achieve its goals, and bring a *network* that will build and not hinder the business. So even though your technical skills might be better, the person hired may have proven that he was stronger in another area the employer needed.

JD had never been a delivery driver before, but he had a clean driving record, understood the importance of keeping to a schedule, and had a friendly, joking personality that ensured regular customers would love him. The manager knew he could teach JD to do the paperwork, load the van, and use the GPS system, but that personality is hard to find. What hard-to-find quality, attitude, or skill can you offer an employer so you stand out from the crowd? To find it, either start with your unique strengths and determine which employers need one or more of them, or start with the job you want and determine how you can meet a need of the employer's that is often lacking. It doesn't have be an extraordinary strength, just one that is needed and uncommon—a manager who can inspire workers to give their best and can create a positive work environment even in tough times, a customer service agent with a great memory for names and faces so returning customers feel important, or an administrative assistant with a vast network who can get things done quicker or at a lower cost.

It's important not just to stand out, but to stand out for the right reasons. What is sought after in one job may not be valued in another. For example, reputable employers want creative marketing executives, not creative accountants. "Patient listening" is a virtue for social workers, not call center operators who work on volume. What strength can you offer that the other two or three hundred applicants can't or wouldn't think to offer? If you're not sure, ask your previous employers what they appreciated most about you, or your friends and family what they think are some of your greatest strengths. Then determine which employers need those things and target them. Or ask industry insiders what qualities, attitudes, or skills are most difficult to find in the field you want to work in, or what employers often complain about regarding people who do the job you desire. Remember, employers dip into their profits because they think the person they're hiring can solve a problem, make them money, or meet an unmet need.

A single hard-to-find quality, attitude, or skill can tip the scales in your favor, as long as it's supported with proof that you can meet the employer's other needs as well. If JD hadn't had a clean driving record or was unable to lift heavy boxes, his hard-to-find personality alone could not have gotten him hired. So it's important that you develop unique proof that you can meet the employer's top three to six needs in each area of PADMAN. This will give you more than twenty targeted selling points for why an employer should hire you!

There are four ways to transform generic selling points into proof that you are uniquely qualified for a particular job. They are not necessarily new or revolutionary, but they are often overlooked. To stand out you must give Facts about your accomplishments, clearly Demonstrate that you naturally possess what an employer needs, offer Credible References to vouch for you, and tell Stories that paint a picture of you doing the job well. We'll teach you how each of these four techniques can make you stand out from the crowd, but first let's look at three important principles to make sure your selling points prove you can do the job:

1. Your selling points must be specific. Everyone the employer interviews will say he or she is hardworking, dependable, and good at the required tasks. If you don't offer specific evidence from your own experience, you will sound like everyone else. To stand out from the crowd, enhance your generic selling points with the four techniques in the chapters ahead.

2. Employers are most comfortable with verifiable proof from paid work history and formal education. But if your work history or education isn't very strong, don't despair. Evidence can be found in lots of less traditional places, too. Chapter 9 will show you how to pull verifiable proof from your whole life.

3. It's only proof if the employer buys it as evidence that you can do the job. So be prepared to offer supporting evidence and follow the rules we'll give you for using transferable skills.

In the next few chapters, not only will we teach you our four techniques to transform your generic selling points, but we will also show you how to use them so you stand out whether you're conducting a traditional front door job search or cleverly looking for a side door. Remember, side doors can be used to find jobs in both in the Open and Hidden Markets, but front door approaches are only effective in the Open Market. (If you don't remember what these are, see Chapter 1.) Follow our advice and you will stand out from the crowd, rather than being screened out with the crowd.

5

Stand Out from the Crowd by Giving Facts

> ➤➤ **FACTS SPEAK FOR THEMSELVES**
>
> How would you choose between a dozen applicants who all told you they were dependable, trustworthy, hardworking, and good at the job? What if one offered Facts about her related accomplishments? *I'm dependable* could become *I missed only 3 working days in 5 years.* Trustworthiness could be proven by sharing that *Although I wasn't a manager, I was regularly given a key to the store and asked to close up and make nightly deposits.* And hardworking could be quantified by saying, *I increased sales by 50% in my first 9 months.* She would stand out.
>
> Quantifying an accomplishment with details that can be verified turns it into a *Fact.* No two people will have the exact same Facts, so when you use your quantified accomplishments on applications and résumés, over the phone and Internet, and in interviews, you are showing your uniqueness. If you worry that using them sounds like bragging, think again! It's not bragging. It's giving employers the Facts they need to decide that you're a wise investment. Employers tend to believe that if you've done it before you'll do it again—for them.

We were visiting an employer when his fax machine beeped and spat out three résumés from the local trade school. They were identical, except for the name and address at the top. As he tossed them in the trash, he said, "When will they learn that boiler-plate résumés aren't helpful, and I don't have time to interview everyone!" Those applicants could have changed the outcome if they had added unique, quantified accomplishments to their résumés. Not sure you have any unique, relevant accomplishments? We bet you do and we'll help you find them. For now, let's take a closer look at how you can transform your selling points into Facts so employers see you can do the job. Here are some examples and how you can verify them:

Offer Proof of Proficiency. *I'm a certified nurse's assistant . . . In my previous job, I was rated "excellent" or "outstanding" in my performance evaluations for team work . . . I have a degree in accounting . . . I'm a licensed builder.* Come prepared to show the paperwork that proves it.

Provide a List. *I can read, write, and speak fluently in English, Spanish, and French . . . I'm proficient in the entire Microsoft Office Professional Suite, plus Adobe Illustrator, InDesign, and Flash . . . I can do all basic car repairs, including changing and rotating tires, changing spark plugs, and checking and changing fluids, filters, belts, and batteries.* Come prepared to take a test, demonstrate any one of the skills, or provide Credible References who can verify each skill.

Use Numbers or Percentages. *I have 4 years' experience in marketing . . . I supervised 9 staff . . . In my last job, I handled approximately 75 calls an hour with a wait time of less than one minute . . . I decreased returns by more than 15% in 9 months . . . I nearly doubled the number of positive responses within one year . . .*

I exceeded targets by more than 20% within 2 months of training. Come prepared to show the paperwork that proves it. If you don't have documentation to prove the numbers, make a conservative guess, and use words like "almost," "approximately," "nearly," and "more than" to ensure your previous employers or customers will agree that your claim sounds accurate if your perspective employer inquires.

Use Comparisons (to an Industry Average, Other Workers, etc.). *I graduated in the top 10% of my class . . . I became proficient in QuickBooks in half the time it took others on my team . . . I was Employee of the Month twice last year . . . I have been among the Top 10 Salespeople for 3 years running . . . Our team was #1 or #2 every month for 32 months . . . I completed the trainer's certificate in 18 months, rather than 2 years.* Have either the paperwork or a Credible Reference who can validate these claims.

Notice how each Fact that uses numbers, percentages, or comparisons also provides a time frame. The time frame is important because it tells the employer whether or not to be impressed. For example, increasing sales by 50 percent in the first six months is much more impressive than having done it over six years. Carrying six plates at one time is impressive. Carrying six plates one at a time is not.

Once you have quantified your accomplishments and added a time frame, ask others to read them to make sure they don't sound too good to be true. If you sound too good to be true, the employer may either think you're lying or wonder why you're unemployed and assume the worst. To avoid this problem, adjust how you present the accomplishment. For example, *I increased sales by 400% in one year* would be more believable, and still impressive, if it were expressed as *I increased sales by $280,000 in one year,* or *I more than doubled sales in my first year.*

➤ **DID YOU KNOW?**

Many employers rely on a combination of what you say, what you do, what you show them, and their gut instinct, rather than actually calling references to check your Facts. So be sure your actions match your words.

Each Fact takes on a slightly different form when used in writing, during cold calls, or during an interview.

In Writing (on Paper or Online). Use brief bulleted statements, rather than full sentences, so employers can see, at a glance, that you have what they need.

- Almost 3 years experience as an Administrative Assistant.
- Very dependable: Missed only 3 days in 4 years.
- Proficient in the current MS Office Professional Suite, QuickBooks, PhotoShop, InDesign, DreamWeaver, Flash, and several Internet search engines and ISPs.

During Cold Calls (Over the Phone or in Person). Keep these Facts short, so you can list three in one breath. This allows you to share all three before giving the employer a chance to screen you out. The employer can always ask additional questions, after agreeing that he needs your skills. It sounds like:

I have almost three years' office experience, and I'm very proficient on the computer and Internet, plus I'm extremely dependable—on my last job, I missed only three days in four years. Could you use someone with my skills?

During an Interview. As you craft these Facts, remember that you'll be talking to someone. Make the Facts sound conversational, but keep them brief and to the point. Sharing a Fact often leads to being asked for a more detailed explanation or a story. As with any good answer, be sure to practice sharing your Facts in front of others before the interview. In response to the question, *Why should I hire you?* it sounds like:

> *I would say that the three top reasons are . . . (thoughtful pause) that I'm very dependable. In fact, on my last job I missed only three days in four years. It was my dependability and ability to meet deadlines that my last boss seemed to appreciate most. Also, the three years I spent as an administrative assistant in a very busy office taught me good time management, the importance of being organized and always working ahead, and how much fun it is to be a part of a team. Lastly, I'm very good with computers and the Internet. As you can see by my résumé, I know all the programs in the Microsoft Office Professional Suite, as well as QuickBooks and several web-design programs. I'm lucky because I find learning new programs fun and easy. What software do you currently use?*

Ending an answer with a question is a great way to direct the employer toward additional selling points you want to mention, create a conversation, show interest, and build a relationship with the interviewer. Remember, when all else is equal, the most common deciding factor is who the interviewer feels most comfortable with.

Since employers have lots of needs, you should have lots of Facts you can use to prove you'd be great at the job. However, only the two or three that are of greatest value to the employer or most difficult to find will become your *key message*. Create your key message by listing the accomplishments or qualities you want the employer to associate with your name and repeat to others when talking about you—*Lilly's the one who can type 85 words per minute, designed that really creative website, and had that great reference from Mr. Jones . . . Dave's the guy who landed the $6 million contract and resolved that difficult union negotiation for XYZ company.* Memorize your key message so it becomes a natural response to various questions like, *Tell me about yourself,* or *Why should I hire you?* Use your key message and all your accomplishments to market yourself throughout your job search, whether using the front door or a side door.

A FRONT DOOR APPROACH: BENDING THE RULES SO YOU GET NOTICED

It's reasonable to think that following the rules is the most effective way to get hired—but it's not. Most job seekers follow the rules by going through the *front door* to submit their application or résumé, then joining the dozens, or hundreds, of other applicants waiting to be contacted for an interview. This is not ideal. However, if you're going to use the front door, let us give you some tips on how to bend the rules so you can get noticed.

Using Facts will improve your front door job search as you highlight your accomplishments rather than past job descriptions. Employers initially spend less than twenty seconds determining if you can meet their needs, so make it easy for them to find the details they need. Don't hide those details under a lot of irrelevant or unhelpful information. Here are some tips for how to do this using the front door's primary marketing tools—résumés and applications.

Résumés. Don't use the same résumé for every job. Tailor it to the target position or type of work by focusing on that employer's PADMAN. Listing skills the employer doesn't need only buries the ones you want her to notice. Use the employer's terminology throughout the résumé because the initial screen out is often based on a search for keywords and conducted by a computer or a junior clerk. At the top of the page add the heading *Summary of Qualifications* or *Highlight of Experience* and list the four to six Facts that will impress *that* employer most. The list will probably include accomplishments from previous related jobs, any specialized training or related degrees, your years of experience in the field (if impressive), work-related awards (Salesman of the Year), work-related honors (president of an industry association), or civic honors (membership on an important city commission) that demonstrate a positive network. If these are impressive, in less than twenty seconds the employer knows you are a keeper.

When deciding whether to list your education or experience next, ask yourself which will impress your target employer more,

---

SAMPLE
HIGHLIGHT OF EXPERIENCE

- More than 10 years of progressive management experience in the food manufacturing industry.
- Oversaw the modernization of a 60,000 sq-ft plant to make it more environmentally sound and cost efficient.
- Generated more than $3.5 million in new business for a start-up company in its second year.
- MBA from Stanford University.
- Type 85 wpm with high proficiency in all Microsoft Office programs.

and put it first. Under *Education* list your most impressive related degrees or training first, even if you completed other degrees or training more recently. You don't have to date your education, especially if you don't want to give away your age. You do, however, have to date your work experience. Start with the most recent and work your way back ten years. Any experience more than ten years old is usually considered out-of-date and ignored, so don't waste the space listing it.

☞ TAKING A PAGE FROM BUSINESS . . .

Incorporate "teasers" into your résumés, cover letters, and spontaneous letters by sharing a Fact about an accomplishment without telling employers exactly how you did it—*Decreased lost or damaged merchandise by 45% in 6 months using an innovative staff participation scheme . . . Increased productivity by 28% during first 18 months by implementing new management techniques.* Make them interview (or hire) you to get the details.

If you use the heading *Recent Work History* or *Relevant Work History*, employers will know you have additional experience that is not listed. Remember your résumé is a marketing tool, not a record of your work history! For each job, don't just list the tasks you did. Employers already know that a secretary types and an account manager meets with customers. Tell them what you accomplished or how well you did it by offering Facts—how fast you type, the positive results of your meetings with customers, how many staff you managed, how big the project budget was. They want to know the results of your efforts and if you have the skills to do the job. So highlight the skills your new employer will need, but don't lie. Your unique accomplishments are enough to make your résumé different from every other applicant's.

Keep your résumé to one or two pages. If that doesn't convince an employer to interview you, more won't. Many employers put long résumés in a "read later" pile, which often never gets read. Keep it short by using bulleted phrases rather than full sentences or paragraphs.

When formatting your résumé, make your name larger than anything else on the page (14- to 16-point type). After all, your résumé is a marketing tool. If you have a second page, create a footer including your name and phone number so employers will know whose résumé the page belongs to if it gets separated. Keep the text at a readable size for older eyes (11- to 12-point). Don't rely solely on spell check. Have someone else read your résumé for typos, wrong words, missed periods, extra spaces, and so forth. Remember, employers assume your résumé represents your best effort, so if they see silly mistakes, they will assume your work will be even worse.

Lastly, review your résumé for anything that could get you screened out. If you've offered information that could concern an employer, such as group or religious affiliations, your age, dangerous hobbies, and the like, remove it. Do you appear fickle or unreliable because you hopped from job to job, or field to field? Do you appear overqualified, underqualified, or as if you should be applying for a different job altogether? If so, use a skills résumé format and tailor it for the specific job you want as described in Chapters 9 and 10. If you are using a skills résumé format, don't send it to recruiters or headhunters without first talking to them personally. Most receive so many résumés that they only consider chronological résumés that have no screen outs. Skill résumés are more effective with small to midsize companies, and the good news is that more people are getting hired in small to midsize companies than in large companies.[1] If your career took a downward turn in responsibility, or you have unexplained gaps in your work history or education, create a skills résumé to give to employers at the interview, but use a spontaneous letter or other side door to get the interview. In Chapter 16, we'll show you how to respond to questions about these issues.

Whether using front doors or side doors, every job seeker needs to have a good résumé to give an employer when requested. Just remember that unless your résumé is exceptional, there are better ways to get interviews.

Applications are tools designed by employers to quickly highlight all the reasons they should screen you out. Online applications are the worst because they are initially reviewed by computers, not people. Here are four general tips to reduce screen outs: (1) Use employers' exact terminology—their keywords; (2) write N/A (not applicable) for illegal questions or those that do not apply to you, rather than leaving them blank; (3) write "negotiable" when asked about salary expectations, so you don't look too expensive or undervalued; and (4) fill gaps in your work history with independent employment if you're doing consulting or odd jobs for various "customers," education (classes or workshops attended, self-study, or private tutoring), or nonpaid work as described in Chapter 9. To stand out from the crowd, answer questions with Facts about your related accomplishments and be sure your key message is obvious.

If you are using an online application, find out the questions ahead of time. Ask others who have completed the application what questions were asked, or if they will keep track of the questions and the allowed word count for you as they complete it—perhaps a friend or family member who is not as concerned about getting hired as they are about helping you. Then create a separate Word document with the questions and your answers before you begin. This will allow you to plan your answers so you can strategically include all the relevant Facts that will get you hired.

It will also give you the opportunity to do a spell check, have others review your answers, count the characters (often you are limited to how many words you can use to answer each question), and edit as needed.

Once you are happy with the answers, you can cut and paste the information into the electronic form, saving you time. (Some online applications have a time limit.) If the application does not allow you to cut and paste, you can quickly reenter the information from your copy. Always reread the answers you retype to check for typos. Once you have created a set of answers for one employer, they can be adapted for future online applications and used to help you prepare for your interview.

Lastly, one good aspect of many online applications is that they focus on assessing the skills and knowledge needed for the job, rather than just your past work history. If you have strong transferable skills, it should come through in your answers.

Our best advice regarding applications is to use a side door first so the employer sees you as a person, not a piece of paper. Even for national companies that have a central clearinghouse for applications, the local manager often has some discretion or influence over who is interviewed. In small to midsize companies the manager often has a lot of discretion. Second, do not lie on any application—even if you know telling the truth will get you screened out. It's a legal document. If you get hired by lying, many companies have a policy that you must be terminated once it's discovered, even if your manager wants to keep you. If you worry that the truth is getting you screened out, that is one more good reason not to use applications. Market yourself to local, small or midsize companies where you can use a side door to highlight your unique strengths or submit your résumé. Résumés can hide many barriers because you choose the format and are not required to answer questions about criminal convictions, major health issues, being fired, and so on, until you are interviewed.

A SIDE DOOR APPROACH:
SPONTANEOUS CONTACT

Side doors are techniques for meeting and impressing the person who can make the final decision, all before you submit your résumé or application . . . and most times, before you even ask for a job. For many positions that you are qualified to do, you can casually meet and talk to the business owner or manager—as a customer, the friend of an employee or associate, a volunteer, a fellow professional in the field or a member of an association, a person doing research, a participant at civic events, or in dozens of other ways. This is especially true for small and midsize companies, and almost always the case in customer-facing businesses. But we must warn you, side doors are not a passive approach. They require a real effort, but that's why managers like them— they want to hire people who make a real effort. It's also the reason most job seekers don't use them. It feels safer to do what everyone else is doing and hope you get lucky—but that isn't how luck works.

One type of side door that relies heavily on Facts is spontaneous contact. Through this door, you contact employers out of the blue, present your key message, and ask if they can use someone with your unique qualities, attitudes, or skills. Do *not* ask if they are hiring or have a job opening—the answer to those questions is often no, even if they do have a position available. Why? Because they fear your main concern is getting a paycheck, rather than making them more profitable. A company's reason for taking on new staff is their belief that it can make them more profitable, if they hire wisely.

➤ DID YOU KNOW?

Saying things like, *I'm looking for work*, or *I'm unemployed and could start immediately*, or *Can I send my résumé or fill out an application?* sounds like your only concern is yourself. To get an interview, replace them with compelling reasons (your key message) to request your résumé, talk with you further, or schedule a meeting.

Spontaneous contacts can be used with companies who are recruiting from the Hidden Market, as well as for jobs listed in the Open Market. As with all side doors, when you use this one in the Open Market, never mention the job advertisement. Instead behave as if you spontaneously decided to ask if you could be a beneficial resource to the employer. This will help you be seen as a talented candidate who wants to join the employer's team, rather than someone who just needs a job. Focus on presenting yourself as a "resource person," as suggested in Chapter 14. Here are some examples of spontaneous contact.

Spontaneous Letter. This is a letter you write directly to the decision maker by name, not just title. Briefly share the top four to six reasons you would be an asset—examples of your accomplishments, praise from past employers, or an explanation of why you want to work in *this* job or *this* company. Again, do not ask for a job. Instead, end by asking if the employer values these skills and qualities, and believes you would be an asset to the team. Give him your contact information, encourage him to visit your LinkedIn profile or your website to learn more, and let him know when you will follow up if you have not heard back. Keep it to one page. Do not include your résumé. *Not* including your résumé increases the likelihood that the decision maker will deal with your letter, rather than pass it to HR, where it's more likely to get screened out.

➤➤ **DID YOU KNOW?**

Your LinkedIn profile can serve as an online résumé. Write it so it markets you for the job, then refer to it in your email signature and on spontaneous letters. It's a great way of saying, "Look at my résumé" without actually sending your résumé.

Rene wanted to respond to a blind job advertisement from a local hospital. Using the information in the ad, she chose accomplishments that proved she could meet the employer's needs and included them in her letter, without ever mentioning the ad. She highlighted a couple of unique qualities, including her experience with a new machine that many hospitals hoped to get in the future, and her contacts with other specialists in the field. She also encouraged employers to view her LinkedIn profile, which was designed to market her for the job. Because the advertisement was blind, she addressed one letter to the decision maker at each of the three hospitals in her area, and individualized it by explaining why she wanted to join that particular team or what impressed her about that hospital. She ended by requesting a phone meeting to discuss how she could benefit each employer, and mentioned that she would call on Friday if she hadn't heard back. After she was hired, Rene learned that there were more than three hundred applicants for the job and that her letter landed her a spot on the short list for interviews. Here is another example of a spontaneous letter:

Sample Spontaneous Letter

M&J Property Management
555 South Main Street
Anytown, CA 92708

Dear Gordon,

I recently visited a property of yours at 4th & Elm, and was impressed by its quality. On further investigation I discovered that M&J has an excellent reputation not only for quality properties, but also for great customer service. I share your belief that praise from customers is the most effective form of marketing, and that paying attention to the little things can make the difference between being average and excellent. Too often, people can't be bothered with details; however, it's one of my greatest strengths.

I understand that M&J generally promotes from within, but I am hoping that my unique mix of skills and similar attitudes will persuade you to add me to your team. I recently graduated from the Art Institute in Interior Design; the quality of my work can be viewed at www .perfectplaces.com. Plus, I have a real-world understanding of the property field because I spent years helping my father remodel old homes and sell them. I was responsible for basic bookkeeping, costing-out jobs, negotiating with vendors, obtaining required permits, designing job flow plans, and meeting with customers. I even learned to paint, hang wallpaper, and perform basic repairs to my father's exacting standards. Most important, I am eager to learn from the best and to be a part of a company that takes pride in its work.

If these are qualities you value, I welcome the opportunity to meet and discuss how I can contribute to your team. I can be reached at 714-555-0986.

Sincerely,

Ima Worker

Spontaneous Emails. These are similar to letters, just shorter, with your selling points bulleted. Again, they are sent directly to the email address of the manager you want to work for, not to HR or a general company inquiry box. Be careful, because in the Open Market spontaneous letters and emails can be redirected to HR by astute secretaries who filter their boss's mail. This is particularly true if you include your résumé, so don't!

In the Hidden Market your approach online must be less direct. You want to briefly share the hard-to-find skill, attitude, or quality you offer, and make an inquiry that compels a response, without asking for a job:

Hello, Mr. Howard: I was told that you might help me with some information. For more than ten years I have successfully worked both sides of the counter—technical and sales. As a leader in the field, where do you see our industry still holding its own? Recently, my shop moved offshore. I love this field and hope to stay in it. Any information would be greatly appreciated.

Don't expect a response from every employer, but to the few who do respond, send a thank-you email with a bit more information about your skills. Now the conversation has begun. Every couple of weeks, send a brief update and occasionally request the employer's opinion in order to keep the conversation going. Don't give up. Employers are often busy and your emails are not their priority. But your polite persistence can lead to an interview and a job.

Spontaneous Internet Connection. For less accessible decision makers, craft LinkedIn and Twitter profiles that position you as a valuable resource and then invite them to connect. If they accept, review their profile and send a brief and friendly greeting. Do not mention that you are looking for work, and don't ask for anything. If they reply, continue the online interaction, presenting yourself as a talented, resourceful person who is interested in the decision maker's work. Be sure every tweet, message, and post shows the qualities, attitudes, skills, knowledge, and connections needed to impress this person. To continue the contact, send another brief, positive message within the next two weeks via LinkedIn, Twitter, or the employer's blog asking a short question or making a comment regarding one of their posts.

Once a connection is established, you may even suggest a phone conversation to discuss something the decision maker wrote, get her opinion on a question you have, get her take on a blog article you are planning to write or a project you are working on, or discuss possible collaboration on a project. Don't be in a hurry to ask for a job. Be sure the decision maker sees your value to his company before asking. If he doesn't reply, wait a week or two then try to engage him again. You initial contact may have come when the decision maker was particularly busy—polite persistence does pay off. Meanwhile, keep an active online presence, and search for additional information you could use to engage the person.

Spontaneous Phone Calls. Because this side door is commonly used, employers have tightened security. It's harder than ever to get directly to the employer. Receptionists are trained to transfer you to HR if you don't have the manager's name. If you have her name, secretaries are often trained to transfer you to voicemail. Even if you have the manager's cell phone number, employers regularly screen calls.

Here are a few tips that may help. Find the manager's name on the company website, industry association membership lists, or the Internet, or ask someone who works for the company. If you call during lunch, the relief receptionist is often more willing to give out a decision maker's name or connect you to his office. If you talk to the manager directly, refer to him by name. Introduce yourself, quickly share the top three reasons you would be an asset to his company, and ask if he can use someone with your abilities. Remember, do not ask if the manager is hiring or say you are looking for a job, keep the focus on how you can help them. Compare what you say to Randy's script:

> *Hello, Mr. Jackson, my name is Randy Myer. I have more than ten years' experience in bookkeeping. I'm proficient in several accounting programs including NetSuite and Peachtree. Plus, I have a proven history of saving my employer money by finding more cost-effective vendors and reducing service fees paid. Could you use someone with my skills?*

➥ DID YOU KNOW?

How a person introduces herself on her voicemail message or when answering the phone tells you whether you should refer to her by her full name or first name only. If the message begins "Hi, this is Elisabeth," use her first name. If she answers "Mrs. Smith speaking," then use this name.

Keep it brief; the manager is busy. If she needs your skills, she will usually ask questions. If she doesn't need your skills, ask if she knows someone who does. Regardless, thank her for her time and move on. If you get the manager's voicemail, use the script and speak as if you were talking with him directly. At the end of your message, repeat your name and leave your phone number. If the manager needs your skills, he'll return your call. If you follow our advice and give managers a reason to talk to you, an average of one in ten will ask to hear more, request a résumé, or agree to meet with you to discuss how you could benefit his business. If you took an hour and made twenty calls, on average, you'd generate two phone or in-person interviews during that hour.

Spontaneous Walk-in. This can be used anywhere the public has direct access to a company's manager, such as hotels, restaurants, stores, insurance companies, brokerage houses, employment agencies, print shops, child care centers, gyms, schools, and more. As a customer you can informally impress the manager with your hard-to-find quality, attitude, or skill *before* mentioning, *This seems like a great place to work. How does someone get on the team here?*

This side door can be used in both the Open and Hidden Market. Josh loved the outdoors, and knew a lot about his local countryside. He noticed that a large outdoor sports store in town was hiring. Rather than submitting his résumé like everyone else, he got the name of the store manager and learned that he usually worked on the floor for several hours each morning. As a customer, Josh walked up to the manager and started a conversation by asking about a nearby product. During the conversation, Josh casually showed his knowledge of other products, a variety of outdoor sports, and local trails and fishing holes. He also demonstrated an ease for engaging strangers, a willingness to be helpful, and a pleasant personality. Without mentioning that he knew he was talking to the manager, Josh ended the conversation by saying, "This is a great store. It must be a great place to work. How does someone get a job here?" Josh started work a week later.

Missy wanted to work in a clothing shop, but no one was advertising openings. Her hard-to-find quality was her natural neatness. What store manager doesn't want staff who pick up after customers without being told? She began visiting stores she wanted to work for. As she meandered toward the back counter, Missy spent several minutes re-hanging or folding clothes so the racks looked neat. All the while, she chatted happily with customers, commenting when something looked good on them. When she reached the back counter, she asked for the manager and shared her top three accomplishments. ("Hi. I'm Missy. I have a year of customer service experience, know a lot about shoes, and enjoy both assisting customers and preparing merchandise for the floor.") Then she asked if the manager could use someone with her skills. Regardless of whether the manager said yes or no, Missy would thank her, then again tidy up as she left and give a friendly wave as she walked out the door. Note that she didn't include her tidiness among the Facts about herself. It's a selling point that's more powerful if a manager notices it on her own. If the manager said no, Missy planned to visit the shop again during the next ten days as a customer, repeating the process and casually inquiring of the manager if anything had come available. Her polite persistence and unique skill paid off, and within a month she was working.

This technique doesn't only work for retail or lower-level jobs. Michael had successfully managed his own investments for years. He found it exciting and enjoyed keeping his knowledge and skills current. When the global company he worked for laid off more than four thousand staff, he took early retirement and decided to pursue a career as a broker. He called a small, well-respected brokerage house, explained that he had a substantial portfolio, and requested an appointment with the owner. During the meeting, the owner was impressed, but surprised that Michael would want someone else to manage his portfolio. Michael pleasantly explained that due to his success, many of his associates asked him for financial advice, and he realized that being a broker was something he would be good at and enjoy. He then shared that he was impressed with the house, and asked if the owner could use someone with his skills and contacts. A deal was struck and the house helped Michael get the required licenses to start his new career.

Sharing Facts about your accomplishments is a great way to prove you're the right person for the job. Do your résumé, cover letter, spontaneous letter, and key message make you stand out, or sound like everyone else?

 QUICK TIPS FOR FACTS

- All selling points start with the employer's needs. If the employer doesn't need it, the Fact isn't a selling point.
- Identify specific accomplishments that prove you can meet each need.
- Quantify each, using numbers or percentages, comparisons, proof of proficiency, or lists.
- Give a time frame (daily, in the first three months, over two years) whenever possible, so the employer is impressed with how quickly it was accomplished.
- Be sure each Fact is true and verifiable either with paperwork or a credible reference.
- Make sure it sounds believable.
- Use Facts to market yourself in writing, during cold calls, and in interviews, when accessing employers through both the front door and side door.
- Memorize your key message—the two or three Facts that are most impressive and valuable to the employer. Use it repeatedly.

6

Stand Out from the Crowd by Demonstration

> **SEEING IS BELIEVING**

What are you more likely to believe, something you see for yourself or something you're told about? For most of us, seeing is believing. That is why Demonstration is one of the quickest ways to get hired. Employers watch you do the very things they need. When they observe you taking a typing test, they know how fast and accurately you type. When they see samples of your work, or watch you give a presentation, cook a meal, or write computer code, they can see for themselves the quality you offer.

But Demonstration goes beyond these typical displays; it includes *everything* you say and do. An applicant who charms the receptionist and makes the interviewer comfortable is "good with people," even if he has never been paid for it. A person is perceived as forward-planning when she comes to the interview having done the needed research and thought through how she can benefit the company. Someone who says she's reliable, but arrives four minutes late is not reliable. And if you say you're hardworking, but received mediocre grades in school, were never promoted, or were the first one laid off, the evidence suggests that you actually do only enough to get by. What do your actions and attitudes demonstrate?

Employers believe that what they see you do in front of them is what they are buying. That's why Demonstration remains the easiest way to prove that you have the image they want, the skills they need, the attitude and motivation they are looking for—all the qualities of their PADMAN. There are a lot of traditional ways to demonstrate value, but there are also lots of creative ways to stand out this way—don't limit yourself. Tabitha was invited for a second interview as a pastry chef at a new, chic restaurant on the Riverfront. She knew that all of the finalists would be asked to cook from the restaurant's menu during the interview, but she wanted to stand out. So, to demonstrate her artistry and commitment to doing the extra, she brought samples of two recipes she had created . . . a beautiful white chocolate mousse garnished with edible wild flowers, and the most amazing low-fat apple and walnut breakfast bread. It worked. What hard-to-find quality, attitude, or skill could you demonstrate, so you stand out from the crowd? A waitress could memorize the menu before the interview. She'll be expected to do it once she's hired, and it demonstrates her commitment to *that* restaurant. A salesperson could create a sales pitch, complete with PowerPoint presentation and an investor's prospectus to show why the employer should "buy" him. An animal trainer could bring a laptop and video of her successfully training animals.

Employers often orchestrate a Demonstration. They may ask you to come prepared with a presentation or they may want you to take a test. They may conduct a group interview to see how social you are, what role you naturally play on a team, if you can group problem-solve, what type of leader you are, and so on. Without warning, they may ask you to sell them an old calculator to see your sales skills and how well you think on your feet. They may playact a fight between staff, or project a negative attitude to see how you respond. They are looking for proof that you can do what you say you can do . . . in every area of PADMAN.

Demonstration is not always intentional. In fact, what you do unintentionally—your helpfulness while waiting for your interview, your unflappable responses to stress questions, and your professional demeanor—is often what employers trust most. And if you demonstrate qualities they don't want—being late, unprepared, a know-it-all, or rude, acting desperate or having poor hygiene or questionable friends—they will assume this is the real you. Davy wanted to demonstrate his creativity and web-design skills, so he directed employers to several websites he had designed. Among them was a porn site, which caused most employers to question his judgment. What actions or attitudes have you demonstrated in the past that may have gotten you screened out—shyness, arrogance, apathy, disorganization, reluctance to do things their way, anger, or something else? Being aware of these traits is the first step in acting differently. It's unrealistic to expect a shy person to become outgoing, but she could smile, make eye contact, and say hello. An arrogant person will not become self-deprecating, but he could talk less about himself and show more interest in others. Those who resent authority won't enjoy being told what to do, but they could equate saying "okay" with getting a paycheck and a promotion. Think about what you must do to project a more positive quality, and demonstrate that instead.

Demonstration is not only what you do in the interview; it's what you do before and after also. John lost a great job because he rudely stole a parking space from the woman who was about to interview him. Peter's friendly interaction with the front office staff when he dropped off his résumé made him someone they wanted to work with. When hired, he was told their comments had been what tipped the scales. Employers are always observing

and evaluating you. Chantell wanted to demonstrate her professionalism and follow-through, so she emailed or hand-delivered a
thank-you note within an hour of each interview. She also emailed
information the interviewer had shown an interest in, including
details about a software package she had mentioned and samples
of forms she had developed. This showed off her skills and willingness to share what she knows to help the business succeed.

☞ TAKING A PAGE FROM BUSINESS . . .

To ignite or heighten prospective customers' interest, it's common to give them a small sample of what you have to offer. As
a job seeker, what can you give prospective employers that
would ignite or heighten their interest? Many technical experts or
senior-level job seekers put on a consultant's hat and offer their
time and expertise for free or at a discount if it might land them
a permanent job. Both white and blue collar workers can share
great ideas, bring in samples of their work, or even volunteer for
a day. Don't give away *all* your best work. Make them hire you to
get the full package.

A FRONT DOOR APPROACH:
MORE THAN JUST WORDS

The most common front door Demonstration is taking a temp
job, consulting assignment, work trial, apprenticeship, internship, or other on-the-job opportunity to prove you're the right
person for a permanent position. You will be in a great position
to discover the employer's PADMAN and demonstrate daily
that you are a perfect match, but you must be deliberate about
it. It's essential that you treat this opportunity as one very long
interview. Remember, employers are watching you. Give them

reasons to keep you. Prove you match the company's attitude and image. Discover your manager's priorities and help achieve them. Be eager to learn, make others look good, and do the extra. And consistently demonstrate the qualities, attitudes, and skills that will make you a unique asset to the company's team.

Even before you get the temporary assignment, you can begin demonstrating your unique quality, skill, or attitude in order to get noticed by the decision maker. Becky Bean wanted to demonstrate her bold creativity to advertising firms, so she scanned the label from a can of beans into her computer and replaced the information so it became a résumé. It was impressive and memorable enough that she was offered the internship she wanted. Of course, if Becky had wanted to be a paralegal, her "bean can résumé" would *not* have been impressive, because most legal firms value uniformity and attention to detail, not creativity. Remember, for your Demonstration to be effective, the quality or skill you demonstrate must be something the employer values.

A SIDE DOOR APPROACH: SHOW THEN TELL

Getting an interview is often harder then getting the job. That is why show then tell is one of our favorite side doors. Employers are always on the look out for employees who naturally demonstrate qualities or skills they need. That's why hiring great staff away from other businesses is so appealing—the employer has already seen the quality of the work. So if you are working and want a change, treat each customer like a prospective employer. Who knows? Your dream job might just find you. If you are not working, how can you show a decision maker the hard-to-find quality, attitude, or skill before letting him know you are interested in working for him? Perhaps you can get some ideas from these examples of how other people got hired.

Richard, who was seeking a position as an advertising manager, created a website highlighting several campaigns he had designed. He contacted twelve decision makers he wanted to work for. Without mentioning that they were his work, he asked them to critique the campaigns, and offered a $150 fee for their expert opinion. He then followed up with those who rated his work highly. Richard said it was the best $1,800 he ever spent. It not only showcased his design skills, it demonstrated his ability to get his ideas in front of the people who matter.

Wendy wanted to work with the elderly, so she volunteered at a local senior center one afternoon a week. She chose a day the director spent among the guests, and always said a casual hello so he became aware of her. Wendy was happy and friendly, and often stayed late listening to the guests' stories or laughing with them. After three weeks, she approached the director, thanked him for the opportunity to spend time with the seniors, and shared this: "I enjoy this so much that I'd like to make it my career. How would I go about getting a job here?" The director said they weren't hiring, so Wendy asked about other centers of similar quality that might have openings. He said he would think about it. Over the next few weeks, the director noticed how much the guests liked Wendy and offered her a part-time job with the promise of a full-time position when one came available. Note: Employers won't assume a volunteer wants a paid position unless the volunteer tells them. Wait to mention it, until you've proven your worth, and don't expect an answer immediately, because employers must decide if what they are getting for free is worth paying for. So, once you've asked, continue to do quality work while they're thinking it over.

Sandra discovered that the senior manager for the company she most wanted to work for had just been elected president of a local industry association. She joined the association, began volunteering in the association's office two days a week in order to meet the manager, and joined a committee that ensured her unique skills would shine. From the start, she gained a reputation for making the manager/president's term successful. Her efforts paid off. She was offered a job before the year was out.

There are lots of ways you can show then tell the unique value you offer a company. It can be fun to brainstorm with friends about creative ways you could demonstrate that you have what the employer needs. Also, keep your eyes and ears open for opportunities to get in front of the person you want to work for like Sandra did.

 QUICK TIPS FOR DEMONSTRATION

- Think of a dozen ways you can demonstrate qualities your new employer needs. Don't be afraid to be creative.
- Be consistent. Demonstrating the needed qualities, attitudes, and skills is not a one-time affair. Do it whenever you interact with the company.
- Evaluate what your past actions have demonstrated. Determine which you will need to change in order to get hired.

7

Stand Out from the Crowd by Offering Credible References

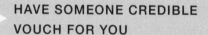

HAVE SOMEONE CREDIBLE VOUCH FOR YOU

Employers tend to believe what others say about you more than what you say about yourself, particularly if the employer views those others as *credible*. There are two groups of people who are credible to employers—those who have an interest in the company's success, and those who value their own reputation and won't tarnish it by vouching for someone the employer might regret hiring. Persuading these people to vouch for you will go a long way in proving you can do the job or learn it quickly. Their recommendation can be the deciding factor in who gets hired.

Not all personal or professional references are Credible References. Often those you list on your applications or résumés are not viewed as particularly credible to employers because they care more about you than about the success of the business. For this reason, the positive things they say are taken with a grain of salt, but the negative things are embraced. After all, it's assumed that you will list those people with the most positive things to say about you.

For better or worse, what *credible* people say about you carries more weight than what you say about yourself. Who do employers consider credible? Whose recommendation do they trust and respect enough to justify investing thousands of dollars in hiring you? Credible References are people the employer believes have the necessary expertise to make a valid judgment and won't lie for you. Determining who has expertise is fairly easy. Determining whom to trust can be trickier. Generally, credible people fall into two groups: first, people who have a vested interest in the company's or the employer's success, such as family and friends, good employees, valued customers, vendors, and business partners; second, people who have little to gain if you are hired, but could lose credibility or damage their professional reputation if the employer feels deceived. This group includes business associates of the employer, college professors, civic leaders, employment specialists who only get paid if you succeed, experts in the field, or your past employers, customers, and subcontractors. The degree of credibility given to each of these people is based on the individual rather than his or her position. For example, Mr. Andrews taught computer programming at a local college and prided himself in helping companies in the industry find great new talent. Consequently, his recommendation was credible. On the other hand, Professor Brown, who hadn't bothered getting to know the local business owners or their needs, gained a reputation for recommending any student who asked. Not surprisingly, his recommendation was not credible.

Here are several groups employers often *don't* trust, or who could do you more harm than good:

- People who have a bad reputation with the employer, including employees who were fired and current employees who cause problems or whose work is below average.

- People who would benefit from the employer's misfortune, such as business competitors.
- People who could gain by lying, such as a current employer who might give a glowing reference to get rid of a bad employee, or a bad reference so she could keep a good one. Yes, it happens!
- People whose only perceived interest is in helping you, like your family and friends.
- People who, by association, generate concerns about your character or stability, such as your psychiatrist, parole officer, case manager, an AA sponsor, or other similar helping professional. These people are credible only if they are also trusted friends of the employer, or are listed as a friend or mentor rather than as your counselor, sponsor, or similar. Ask their permission before redefining your relationship. It could be embarrassing if you call them a friend and they call you a patient.

TOP TIPS FOR CHOOSING AND PREPPING
YOUR REFERENCES

Choose people who are not only credible, but also believe that you'd be great for the job. Help them market you for each job by providing them a copy of your résumé, your key message, a couple of stories that highlight your top skills, and an explanation of why you are excited about the job. You can subtly do this in a letter sent with your résumé or during a conversation. When talking to references who are past employers, subtly remind them of specific things you accomplished while working with them by overtly thanking them for the opportunity to have learned or achieved those things as part of their team. After each successful interview, call or email all your references with a quick update, including the company name and mission, the specific title you are competing for, how the interview went, and your particular strengths for this job with this company. This will make your references part of your sales team.

➨ **DID YOU KNOW?**

When asked to give a reference, people tend to repeat the last thing they heard or discussed about the person (unless it could get them sued). To influence what others share about you, subtly remind them of your accomplishments and positive qualities before the employer calls them.

If you have a poor relationship with a past employer, but believe a positive reference from him could make the difference between getting hired or screened out, start by *never* talking badly about him—even if he deserves it. Employers don't want employees who point the finger at the employer when things go wrong. Instead, focus on what you liked about the company or job—great coworkers, or what you learned or had the opportunity to accomplish. Next, in order to neutralize or improve a negative reference, make amends. Call the employer and apologize for what you did that added to the troubles. Don't expect him to reciprocate. Your goal is not an apology from the employer, it's a job with someone else. Call the supervisor you got along with best to thank her for something positive, briefly acknowledge your fault and what you're doing to correct it, remind her of your good qualities, let her know you are job searching, and ask if she would be a work reference for you—in that order. For Martin, it sounded something like this:

Hi, Jim. It's Martin. I'm calling to thank you for some advice you gave me when I worked for you. Remember how you said that I got along great with people as friends, but I work best on my own? You're right. That's why I'm applying for jobs at the US Forest Service. I'll get to work around people, but most of my work will be done independently. Plus, I love the outdoors, and I'm not afraid of hard work—which you know, because you could always count on me to take an extra shift or stay late when no one else would. And I'll finally get to use my degree in Environmental Science. You know how passionate I am about those issues. Remember I started the company's recycling program? Since you know the quality of my work and what a good match this job is for me, I would like to list you as a work reference. Would that be okay?

A FRONT DOOR APPROACH: RESPONSIVE CREDIBLE REFERENCES

There are two ways Credible References can help—they can be responsive or proactive. A *responsive* Credible Reference is someone who has agreed to respond to the employer's inquiries. He can be a past supervisor, customer, or another person you list on your application and reference sheet who can verify your unique qualities, attitudes, and skills. Most employers ask for three references. If you have only one who is credible, list that one first. Then add other colleagues or friends who can vouch for your character and skills.

Create a separate reference page, formatted to match your résumé, and list the names and contact information for your references. If they are likely to impress the employer, send it with your résumé. If not, bring it to the interview and give it to employers when they ask for it. When asked on an application for your current employer, list a supervisor who is willing to give specific, positive examples of your work with the company—otherwise, give the employer the direct number to HR, which will only verify your start and end date, position, and if you are eligible for rehire. Be sure to contact and prep all references before listing them.

Written statements from Credible References can also be effective if it is obvious that it was the reference's idea and not yours. (Letters of reference from past employers are often taken with a grain of salt because so often managers tell soon-to-be job seekers to write their own letter and they'll sign it.) Daniel had moved to a new city and wanted to work for one of the local newspapers. In his previous job, he had solved a major problem for a printing press manufacturer, which saved them lot of money. They sent him a thank-you letter and a case of steaks. Daniel quoted from this "letter of recommendation" in his cover letter and offered to provide a copy.

You can also share praise from responsive references during an interview, such as *My last supervisor boasted that I was the one person he could count on to be early and stay late*, or *I have a list of satisfied customers who've said they'd be happy to take your call.* Any positive comment about you that is attributed to a specific Credible Reference and can be verified carries more weight than what you say about yourself. So make the effort to find Credible References.

A SIDE DOOR APPROACH: PROACTIVE CREDIBLE REFERENCES

A *proactive* Credible Reference is a person the decision maker trusts, who agrees to call, write, email, or talk with that person on your behalf, without waiting to be contacted by the employer first. Leslie wanted proactive references, so she asked her professor if he knew of any sports programs that could use an assistant coach, then she asked if he would be willing to call them and put in a good word for her. Henry moved to the top of the list when his mentor, who was a golf partner of his prospective employer, put in a good word for him as they talked on the greens. Junior had worked in a resort in the Philippines, but he married an American and immigrated to the States. His wife's friend worked at a prestigious hotel and offered to introduce him to the manager. Junior met her for coffee, after which she orchestrated an informal introduction. Her recommendation resulted in an interview, to which Junior brought his résumé. To use this common side door, identify someone who works for or knows the owner/manager of a company you want to work for. Share with that person your key message for the job and ask if he is willing to introduce you. If they are credible, references like this can tip the scales.

➤ **DID YOU KNOW?**

> The reason people are not promoted is often due to not having anyone credible to champion their promotion. What have you done to make a superior or experts in the field go out of their way to champion you? It is often the deciding factor.

There are lots of ways your Credible References can proactively orchestrate informal "meetings" with decision makers—it's similar to how we set up friends for dates.

• If a Credible Reference knows the decision maker socially, she could organize an introduction by hosting a dinner party or BBQ or inviting you to a community or sporting event.

- If a Credible Reference knows the decision maker professionally, he could introduce you at an association meeting or industry event.
- If your reference works for the decision maker, as in Junior's example, she can arrange to casually introduce you and, in your presence or after you leave, share your key message and mention that you'd be a great addition to the team.

You will land an interview, because of the combination of the Credible Reference's recommendation and your performance on the day you meet the decision maker.

Some of your proactive references may opt for a more direct approach in which they actually help set up an interview. Again there are many ways they can do it. They can simply:

- Mention to the decision maker that they have a friend or colleague they think would be an asset to their company.
- Send an email or letter of introduction sharing your top selling points and offer their personal endorsement of you. This differs from a letter of recommendation, because it's written directly to the person who has the power to hire, from someone they know and trust.
- They can pick up the phone and market you directly to the decision maker, like a headhunter, relying on their relationship to reinforce that the recommendation is based on their belief that you'd be good for the company.

In each of these instances, references share your unique qualities, attitudes, or skills for the job and offer to set up a meeting or arrange to have you call the decision maker directly. Your proactive Credible Reference is giving you access to her network, so make her look good and be sure to thank her. Bring your résumé to the meeting, but don't give it to the employer until he asks for it, or you'll appear pushy or presumptuous.

UNCOVERING YOUR CREDIBLE REFERENCES

If you don't think you have any Credible References, look again. Our guess is that you do. They don't have to be lifelong friends, they just have to be people the employer trusts who are willing to vouch for you. Expand your list to include anyone you get along with. Remember what Malcom Gladwell, author of *The Tipping Point*,[1] said, "People weren't getting jobs through their friends. They were getting them through their acquaintances . . . 55.6% of job seekers saw their reference only occasionally, 28% saw them rarely." Who do you occasionally or rarely see who already works where you'd like to work, has done consulting work for them, or is a business associate, or attends the same church, plays golf, or socializes with a decision maker there—and would be willing to introduce you? Marc was changing fields and did not know many people in the new field. So he attended an industry conference to start building his network and to find potential Credible References. He also gained current industry knowledge and discovered which companies were growing so he could target his job search. Being a temp, intern, student worker, or volunteer can be a great opportunity to impress the people around you so they agree to be a Credible Reference for you.

QUICK TIPS FOR CREDIBLE REFERENCES

- Identify two to four *credible* people who will vouch for your skills, character, and other positive qualities needed for the job you want. Remember, if you are pursuing more than one job title, you will need different résumés, key messages, and perhaps different references.
- Prepare your references to market you.
- If they know the employer, ask them to be proactive by contacting the employer or introducing you directly.
- During the interview, do not "name drop" more than twice, unless you are responding to the employer's questions about who you know. Otherwise, you will appear annoying or desperate.

8

Stand Out from the Crowd by Telling Stories

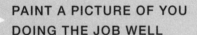

PAINT A PICTURE OF YOU DOING THE JOB WELL

Stories create a snapshot of you doing the job and are often remembered long after the details of your résumé are forgotten. In an interview, stories make your accomplishments come to life and can totally change an employer's perception of you. In fact, interviewers often ask for Stories, when they say, *Tell me about a time when you . . .* or *Give me an example of . . .* Coming to the interview prepared will make your stories more effective, and you more confident.

Stories can also help get you an interview. They can be told by you or a Credible Reference to convince the employer to invite you to talk further. Your Stories will always be unique to you. Learning how to tell them effectively will ensure you stand out for the right reasons.

As you think back on what you've read in this book, what comes to mind? It's likely to be the stories we've told. The same is true for your interview. Interviewers will remember your Stories and be persuaded by them. They often ask for examples of you doing a specific task or demonstrating a specific quality. If you haven't prepared before the interview, you can freeze up, offer weak examples, or say something that gets you screened out. However, if you choose and practice telling your Stories beforehand, you'll appear more confident and qualified.

Here are our top tips for developing effective true Stories. First, the Story must meet an employer need. If the employer doesn't need it, it's not a selling point. Preferably the Story should tell how you solved a problem, saved the company money, or made them money. For example, if the job requires event planning skills, a Story about how you easily handled problems that arose while planning a conference or a fund-raiser would paint a great picture. If you are trying to prove you're detail-oriented, a Story about being the person in the accounting office coworkers turned to when they couldn't find missing pennies or files highlights how you can save the company in staff time and problems with auditors. Vivian wanted to prove her talent for finding creative ways to engage young students in subjects that many find boring and difficult. She told a story about how her students looked forward to math lessons because they were allowed to spread a layer of shaving cream across their desks and use their fingers as the pencil. Their happy, eager attitude made it easier and more fun for her, too.

Second, go beyond the specific incident to the positive results you achieved. Vivan's story was made more effective by sharing the principal's surprise at her student's good test results and positive attitude toward math. Albert was applying to be the head of maintenance at a small industrial complex. With more than ten years' experience in building maintenance, he was skilled in most aspects of the work. However, he realized that "being good on his tools" was not enough to become the head of maintenance. So, to prove he had the problem-solving skills needed to be a manager, he shared a Story about saving his last company more than $50,000 by designing and recommending a preventative maintenance plan. His plan revealed a plumbing problem that could have caused more than $50,000 in damages if it had not been addressed. Repairs took less than a day and cost less than $300 in supplies.

☞ **TAKING A PAGE FROM BUSINESS . . .**

Use the STAR Approach.[1] To create effective Stories, briefly describe the Situation you faced or Task you accomplished, then explain the Actions you took and the positive Results you achieved. Using STAR as your template ensures you select specific stories that highlight accomplishments.

Be sure your Story doesn't include any information that could get you screened out. Prince wanted to tell the owner of a shipping company about the time he stood up to an armed robber in the corner store where he worked. Although this story illustrated that he could be depended on to safeguard the owner's interests, it might have caused concerns about his judgment and possible lawsuits if someone got shot. Before using that story, he had to be sure the employer agreed with him on how to handle robbers. If the employer didn't, he should pick a different story. Lois's dependability was also brought into question when she lied because she didn't think her accomplishments were impressive enough. When the prospective employer called to check the facts, her exaggeration was discovered, her trustworthiness was brought into question, and she was screened out.

Lastly, keep your Stories brief and to the point, only thirty to ninety seconds. Leave the employer wanting more, not wishing you'd shut up. Don't estimate. Time yourself. And remember, you want to create a conversation, so allow the employer to ask you questions if she wants more information. Tell each Story to your friends. Ask them if it proves your point, doesn't cause any concern, and is engaging. Use their feedback to make it even better. Also, ask what follow-up questions they might ask if they were the employer, so you can prepare good answers for them as well. When you think it's ready, tell yourself the Story in the mirror so you can be sure your facial expressions match your message. It might seem strange at first, but it works! Stories are a powerful and memorable way to prove you're the best person for the job.

A FRONT DOOR APPROACH: NOW FOR
THE REST OF THE STORY

Résumés and paper applications don't lend themselves to sharing stories. However, online applications often ask you to *Give an example of a time when you . . .* , which is a request for a Story. Brief Stories (one to three sentences) can also be used in cover letters to highlight a needed quality, skill, or attitude, counter a concern, or show passion for the job, as Melissa did when applying to work as an insurance claims clerk:

> *I know I am new to the insurance industry, but I have five years' office and customer service experience and would really like to work for ABC Insurance. Last year, when my mother was in a serious car accident, the support of your team made*

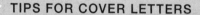

TIPS FOR COVER LETTERS

An effective cover letter will make the reader want to review your résumé and meet the person behind the letter. It should make the reader feel like you're speaking directly to him and allow him to see how you fit into his company. Keep it to one page, and address it to a specific person, not a job title. Feature your key message in your cover letter, but don't waste space making it a repeat of the *Highlights of Experience* section on your résumé. Instead use your cover letter to:

1. Highlight selling points that don't fit smoothly in a résumé. Demonstrate your knowledge of the company, industry trends, and current challenges and solutions by sharing a brief story. Tout valuable or hard-to-find qualities and attitudes with brief examples, perhaps about your passion for a particular issue, your integrity, or as Melissa did, why you really want to work for this company. Draw attention to a valuable network of yours or increase your standing by sharing what your Credible References say about you. The fact that internationally renowned career development expert and bestselling author Richard Bolles[2] named Debra Angel (MacDougall) as one of "six thinkers who have had the most influence on me over the years" significantly increased her credibility.

2. Address concerns that can't be easily dealt with on the résumé. Sergeant Murphy used his cover letter to refute a stereotype that was getting him screened out. You might need to briefly explain what you have done and learned during a recent gap in work experience, or share your motivation to stay in the area even though you have relocated several times. End your cover letter with a clear statement that you look forward to talking with the employer further and will follow up if you haven't heard within a specified time.

Electronic cover letters should be briefer because employers often scan rather than read them. Use concise bullets to highlight key thoughts. As with all of your employer correspondence, have someone proofread your cover letters for typos and grammar, as well as clarity and effectiveness.

a difficult time easier, and their guidance saved me and your company a lot of time and money.

Sergeant Murphy used his cover letter to counter the stereotypes about career marines. After twenty years of military service, he wanted to transition into a counseling position at a university, but the student life staff were concerned that military discipline and university life were incompatible. His cover letter politely and humorously explained that he was not a typical sergeant, and why he could easily relate to students. It resulted in three schools that wanted to meet "the soldier who wrote that letter," and a job offer. Remember, the purpose of a cover letter and résumé is to get an interview so you can offer the proof that will get you hired.

A SIDE DOOR APPROACH: A SUBTLE TECHNIQUE

Stories can be a very effective tool in both the Open and Hidden Markets for impressing decision makers or their gatekeepers to consider you for a position. While searching the web, Eli found a blind ad for an assistant to the senior vice president of a major music label. It was easy to draw Facts from his previous work experience to prove he could meet the qualifications. He also had some unique selling points that would be valuable to this employer. First, his extensive knowledge of music trivia meant he could recognize most artists instantly, but he also possessed the professional grace to never act like a star-struck fan. Also, because artists can be demanding and temperamental, he decided to share a Story from his last job, in which he regularly dealt with foreign customers who were also notoriously demanding and temperamental.

Rather than merely submitting his résumé to the designated website, he wrote spontaneous letters to the assistant to the CEO for each local music label, knowing that as the highest-level assistants, their opinions would carry weight. He didn't write to the VPs directly, because he didn't know which department was hiring. His unstated goal was to have his letter passed to the VP who was hiring, so that person would contact him and request his résumé.

Rob found that Stories were a subtle way to share his greatest strengths with potential employers or Credible References. He used them at social events, such as BBQs, dinner parties, and mixers, or when casually chatting as a customer at companies he wanted to work for. His one caution was in between his stories to ask questions that allowed the other person to also share his or her strengths. This makes it feel like a friendly, open conversation, not a desperate effort to impress. If the other person was reluctant to share, then Rob limited himself to one story. He has used this technique to help him get his last five jobs.

👍 QUICK TIPS FOR STORIES

- Prepare three to six true Stories that paint a picture of you successfully doing a *specific task* the employer needs for the job you want.
- Don't share inappropriate information or lie.
- Keep your Stories to only thirty to ninety seconds. If employers want more information, they'll ask.
- Keep your written Stories to one to three sentences. Yes, a one sentence story is possible, as illustrated earlier.
- Share each of your Stories with several friends and make adjustments.
- Practice each Story in the mirror. Your actions speak louder than you may think.

We've discussed the four ways you can prove you meet the employer's needs so you stand out. Now, let's take a look at where you can draw your accomplishments from, particularly if you are changing fields or transitioning into the business culture from school, the military, full-time parenting, a correctional institution, foreign employment, or similar. You may be surprised at just how many transferable skills you have!

9

A New Take
on Transferable Skills

I f you are changing job titles or fields, you will need to use transferable skills to prove you are qualified for the new job you want. The term "transferable skills" is batted around a lot these days. Traditionally, it refers to skills or knowledge gained in one job that can be used in another, such as a business executive using her real world experience to teach college, or a construction foreman using his field knowledge to prove he would be great as a property inspector.

As with all skills, the value of transferable skills lies in your ability to persuade the employer that they can be used to solve a problem, meet a need, or make the company more profitable. Too often, job seekers think it is the employer's job to find the connection. As employers, we have received hundreds of résumés that made us wonder why the job seekers sent them to us. Many had impressive selling points, but not for the job we'd advertised.

Perhaps the applicants did have skills we needed, but we'll never know because their lack of proof got them screened out in the first round.

To identify your transferable skills, start by identifying the specific knowledge and skills needed by the new employer. If you can prove you meet all those needs relying solely on your paid work history and formal education, great! Do it! If not, add skills gained from other sources. Marco had owned a hospital in South America. When he was forced to flee his war-torn country, he came to the United States. His medical license wasn't recognized in the States, but he used his experience and education to land a job assisting doctors at a clinic in the Hispanic community. After he decided not to pursue an MD in the United States, he began focusing on owning another business that helped people. He noticed that few real estate agents in his area were native Spanish-speakers, and he knew that would make a difference in his community. His professional demeanor, obvious people skills, willingness to learn, and ever-expanding network in the local Hispanic community got him a position with a large real estate company that helped him get his license. In less than three years he put his business management skills to work and opened his own office.

EXPANDING THE DEFINITION OF
TRANSFERABLE SKILLS

Employers believe that if someone else has paid you to do the job, you're more likely to be good at it. That's why transferable skills from your past work and formal education can help you market yourself for a new job. But what if you can do the job, even though you've never taken a class or been hired to do it? Until you offer proof from other sources, you will appear unqualified. So let's expand our definition of transferable skills.

When employers hire you, they get all of your knowledge and experience, regardless of where you gained it. Your unpaid experience could translate into skills employers need, so don't limit yourself. We've coached people who got their best proof from their hobbies, volunteer experience, or everyday life. At sixteen, Gordon was more experienced in car repair than most adults. He had helped his uncle overhaul more than a dozen engines and had done two all by himself—just never as an employee. Luke could create a very impressive website in a couple of nights, and had done it numerous times. He even designed one for a friend's band with videos and music downloads, and another for his mom's consulting business with an e-store and e-zine. Delia was one of the last managers downsized by a large telecommunications company that had laid off hundreds of workers. She decided to change fields and reinvent herself using her paid and unpaid transferable skills. Her new goal was to manage career services for an educational institution. She reworked her résumé, chose fresh references, and crafted her good answer about her transferable skills:

I have more than ten years' experience successfully managing a department. As a manager, I have always been active in helping my staff develop their careers, both within the company and as they move on. I was also involved in the employment transition services offered to my staff when they were laid off. For several years I've also volunteered as an employment coach for people with significant barriers. I think you'll find that my solid work history in the private sector, proven leadership skills, job coaching experience, and passion for the field will serve the college and your students well.

Within four months she had started as career services director at a technical school.

If you limit your proof to paid work and formal education, the employer may never see the talents you could bring. Jason wanted to be an assistant manager in a restaurant. He'd been a cook and a waiter, but never a manager. He believed his life experience and natural talent were enough, so we identified the employer's top needs for the job he wanted, and set out to prove that Jason could meet them. Need by need, we asked him, "Why do you think you can do this? When have you done it before?" Many of his answers came from a single experience: taking over as coach of a community baseball team that had been last in the league for two years. As coach, he revamped practices, corrected mistakes, taught new skills, brought in new talent, and motivated the defeated players. Within a year, he took the team from last to second in the league. He was a great manager! We just had to present it so the employer could connect the skills he used with the team to the skills needed to be an assistant restaurant manager.

Let's look at how you can pull transferable skills and develop powerful Facts, Credible References, Demonstration, and Stories from less traditional sources. Let's start with Facts and Credible References. Here are ten sources of transferable skills you may not have thought you could use, as well as a sample Fact for each, how the skill could be verified, and who could act as a Credible Reference for it. Remember, people are credible because of their expertise, firsthand knowledge of your skill, or relationship with the employer you wish to work for.

- **Volunteer Experience.** *I have painted the exterior of more than a dozen houses. What my customers appreciate most is that I work fast, but I am always careful, and* *clean up after myself.* Provide a list of "happy customers," even if they are neighbors and the elderly shut-ins for whom you did the work for free. Others who could vouch for you include another volunteer, an employee of the organization you volunteer for, or a public official who admires your efforts.

- **Internship or Trial Work Experience.** *I have experience with most office technology, including computers, copiers, fax machines, scanners, video conferencing, LCD projectors, multi-line phones, and teleconferencing.* The fact that you learned it all during a brief internship or work trial does not need to be mentioned until you are asked in an interview. If you gained a mentor through the experience (someone who is an expert in the field, who has chosen to guide you in your career), your mentor can vouch for your skills and will often give you access to his or her contacts.

- **Daily Life.** *I have 2 years' experience caring for an elderly man with Alzheimer's.* The employer doesn't need to know until the interview that the elderly man is your grandfather, and a reference from your grandfather's doctor can verify your skills. To verify skills pulled from your daily life, consider who has seen you use the needed skills, like another parent on the PTA who can vouch for your organizational skills and ability to get the job done, or the plumber who plumbed your new bathroom and noticed how skillfully you had tiled the floor.

- **Hobbies.** *I have been restoring furniture for 10 years. Here's a picture of my work.* Pictures or samples of your work can prove the quality of your skills. Whether your hobby is fixing cars or computers, you can have "customers" you served or someone who shares your hobby testify to your skill.

- **Natural Ability.** *Animals seem to know I am their friend and easily trust me. I'd be happy to volunteer a few days to show you what I mean.* What comes easily to you? What do others ask you to do? You may not think of these as skills, but they are. They are your natural skills.

- **Education.** *I have completed 6 units of Early Childhood Development.* If you haven't completed your degree or your degree isn't relevant to the work you are pursuing, you can still highlight related courses, plus relevant seminars sponsored by past employers. Fellow students who are employed in the field or instructors who are impressed with your industry knowledge, skill, or performance could vouch for you.

- **Self-Taught.** *I have built 6 computers from parts and have upgraded more than 24, receiving nothing but praise from customers.* Self-taught skills can often be proven by taking a test, using the skill in front of employers, showing samples of your work, or having "customers" (often friends and family) vouch for the quality of your work.

Transferable skills can even be pulled from experiences that normally shouldn't be mentioned in an interview. If you, like the people in the examples below, have valuable transferable skills from these nontraditional sources, you can use them. Just be sure to share them in ways that don't raise additional concerns.

- **Community Service or Welfare Program.** *I created a plan that increased day care attendance by 15%, earning*

the company more than $30,000 a year. The director of
the day care center wrote a letter of recommendation
verifying the contribution. In the interview, Shaundra
explained she had been a volunteer, but not that it had
been a government-mandated program.

- **Prison Experience.** *I have 4 years' experience working
  in a very busy industrial kitchen.* Bo didn't state that
  it all happened while he was an inmate, because he
  crafted a good answer for the interview.
- **Residential/Treatment Program.** *I have 10 months'
  experience doing deliveries and pickups in this city, and
  always completed my routes on time.* Matt didn't share
  that the skills were gained as part of his work therapy
  program. He used his work therapy supervisor, not his
  counselor, as a work reference.

Now that you've seen how to pull Facts and Credible References from less traditional sources, let's look at how you can draw
Demonstration and Stories from them. The great thing about
Demonstration is that it doesn't matter where you gained the skill
or quality you are demonstrating, just that employers like what
they see. So, demonstrating skills from less traditional sources is
easy. We once had a client who had never had a paid job and wanted
to work for the Parks and Recreation Department. She impressed
employers using a newspaper article that touted her contribution
as the volunteer coordinator of a highly successful, local festival
and included a picture of her with the mayor. Another client, to
prove his skill with plants, brought a rare and delicate orchid from
the collection he'd cultivated, and left it for the employer as a gift
to make sure he was remembered. No matter where you gained
the skills needed to do the job you want, demonstrate them every
chance you get during the hiring process.

Stories can also come from less traditional sources. To prove she is detail-oriented, a woman told a Story of how she orchestrated all the travel plans for forty-five kids and nine chaperones for a high school choir's thirteen-day European tour. To prove he is conscientious and disciplined, a man shared how in his personal finances he has never been overdrawn or charged a late fee. Another woman who was interviewing as a teacher's assistant for an inner city school explained that she'd spent twenty-two years bringing up six children who had all graduated high school, were drug-free, and supported themselves.

When pulling Stories from your personal life, be careful that they don't seem inappropriate or introduce new concerns. Share them with friends before the interview to make sure you strike the right balance. Cellie's dream was to own a business in the field of animal care, but she knew that to be successful would take more money and business savvy than she currently had. We suggested she begin by working at a local animal rescue center. One of the skills the center required was the ability to calm and manage anxious animals. To discover how Cellie could prove she had this skill, we asked her why she thought she was good at it and when she had done it before. Her wandering examples included:

I've been doing it for years. Locally, I'm known for taking in strays and hurt animals. My neighbors call me if they see one, or even bring them to my house. [This could work, as long as she is not seen as the "scary cat lady" type.]

Animals seem to trust me more than they trust other people, and I understand how to move and speak to help them feel calm and safe. [This is good, but too generic. Let's get specific.]

Right now I have a cockatoo that was given to me by a woman who decided he was too aggressive to keep around her children. I'm socializing him, as I do with most of my strays. One technique I use is water. Cockatoos don't like water, so getting him to trust me when he is in or around water can speed up the process. Every morning when I shower, I bring the cockatoo into the bathroom, hoping he'll join me in the shower. [Whoa! Too visual . . . That's a story that should never be told in an interview. Let's try again.]

There are two wild magpies that live in my front garden. Magpies are notorious for not liking people, but I've gotten them to trust me so much that they will eat out of my hand. [Wow! She's like Snow White.]

In the end, we crafted a Story about Minty and Jelly Bean, the magpies, and a Story of how Cellie socialized a stray puppy that was successfully integrated into a family with three young children.

WHEN *NOT* TO USE AN EXAMPLE OF TRANSFERRABLE SKILLS

We have given you lots of ideas on where and how to find proof that you can do the job, so it may seem that nothing is off-limits—but that is not entirely true. There are two reasons you would choose not to use an example. One, when it creates new concerns, and, two, if you don't want to.

Sometimes specific proof can introduce new concerns. For example, a person who needs to prove she is caring, patient, and resourceful may want to pull proof from her experience caring for her disabled child. It's true that this activity can prove this, but many employers will be concerned that she will also be tired or distracted at work, miss too many days or ask for extra time off, or leave to resume care of the child. Unfortunately, the employer doesn't know how old the child is, how reliable the new caregiver is, or how much responsibility she still has (feels) for the child's well-being, and most won't ask. So this proof may cause more problems than it solves.

The second reason not to use an example is because you don't want to. If proof of a needed quality, attitude, or skill comes from a painful experience, you don't have to use it. Particularly if the negative situation probably won't come up (a juvenile offense that has been sealed or expunged, former addiction, or a struggle with mental illness that doesn't show in your work history). Too often, in an effort to be honest, people turn an interview into either a confessional or a therapy session. Your diploma from the school of hard knocks will not impress employers unless it's clear how it benefits them. They seldom hire people because they feel sorry for them due to a personal crisis, unfair dismissal, divorce, etc. . . . so why share it? However, if that negative situation is going to come up anyway (having been fired, time spent in prison, and so forth), why not turn lemons into lemonade and use it to prove you can meet the employer's needs? At least this way you get to share what you learned and how the employer will benefit from your hard times. Chapter 16 will show you how to address these types of issues.

THE RULES FOR EFFECTIVELY USING TRANSFERABLE SKILLS

We answered the question of where to find your transferable skills. Now let's take a look at the rules for using them. If used correctly, they are very effective. If not, they can make you look as if you don't understand the employer's perspective.

When we told you about Jason, the community baseball coach who wanted to be an assistant restaurant manager, did you think, *That's nice, but an employer is never going to buy his coaching experience as proof that he would be a good manager?* They did! And they will buy your proof, too, as long as you follow these rules. It's easy to do when using paid work and formal education, but can be trickier when using less traditional sources. Most employers would express surprise that someone who grows award-winning tomatoes in their back garden thinks it proves they can run a farm, or that because someone is a parent they think they're automatically qualified to be a preschool teacher. Job seekers who try to make leaps like these do not understand how to use transferable skills. The rules here will help you avoid their mistakes.

Rule 1: Do not assume an accomplishment can be turned into something more than it is. Growing award-winning tomatoes in your garden proves you have the knowledge, skills, and patience to grow award-winning tomatoes (and perhaps other plants). It does not prove that you understand the issues involved with growing them on a mass scale or managing a farm. If you wanted to use this experience to get a job managing a tomato farm, you would need to offer additional proof for the other skills required to run a large farm. Also, being good at a skill doesn't prove you can teach it to others. If you want to teach, you need to prove your ability to transfer information to others. If the primary skill you want to use is growing award-winning plants, you should pursue gardening jobs at specialty nurseries.

Rule 2: You must have done it, and done it well. Just because you have done something as a hobby, or hold a title in your personal or professional life (Mom, football coach, Sunday school teacher, boss) doesn't prove you are skilled at it. Your proof must demonstrate that you can do the thing well. Being a parent doesn't mean you are good with children. If you want to use your parenting experience to prove you are good with kids, you must give specific examples. To prove you are creative and familiar with the needs of children, you could share crafts and indoor activities you designed to entertain your kids on rainy days. To prove that other parents find you trustworthy, you might share how yours is the one house on the block where all the parents allow their kids to spend the night because you are so responsible, and the children have a great time!

Rule 3: Don't make big leaps. Employers won't take the leap from your personal life to your work life, or from one job to another, if it doesn't make sense. So be sure the skill you are trying to prove is actually proven by the activity you describe. Would you hire a teenage girl to watch your children simply because she has been responsibly taking care of the family pet for the last three years? I'm guessing not. But could she use the fact that she has gotten up at 6 a.m. seven days a week for the last three years to walk her dog, and only missed four days when the doctor said she had to stay in bed, to prove that she is dependable and can show up on time in the morning? Definitely!

Rule 4: Don't assume employers know. When pulling skills from your personal life or from a different field of work, don't assume employers know all that is entailed in doing a task, as they would if you mentioned a skill from their workplace. Your proof should describe the skills used to successfully do the task. Stating that you were the chairperson for your class reunion planning committee does not prove you have organizational skills, so describe specifically what you did:

> *I personally negotiated special rates with an airline and four hotels, and organized ground transportation for more than three hundred out-of-town guests. I planned and organized all the arrangements for three unique day-after activities that were*

attended by more than two hundred people. This included select-ing sites, negotiating contracts, collecting payments, arranging transportation, and doing all the crisis management that comes with coordinating a multi-site function. As chairperson, I over-saw the activities of three committees, comprised of 12 people who were responsible for marketing & registration, decorations & nostalgia, and food & entertainment. The reunion received rave reviews from alumni and their families.

Rule 5: Use the employer's language. Paint a picture the employer can relate to before she discovers where you gained the skill. This is easily done by replacing situation-specific language with generic language or business terms. In the example above "300 guests" simply becomes "300 delegates." What other language might you change in that example? For Jason, the baseball coach: "In the first six games our fielding errors went from 40% to 25%," became "Within six weeks, I was able to decrease mistakes in a key area by 15%."

Rule 6: Look for concerns. Once you have prepared your proof, review it for anything that might concern an employer. Andre has had a long and successful career in corporate management, but he wants to make a difference in his community before he retires in ten years. He is pursuing leadership positions in the nonprofit sector, but employers are concerned that the pay and the excitement won't be enough, and that he will soon return to his former career. He could attempt to reduce their concerns by explaining that he is financially comfortable, has always planned to spend the last ten years of his career giving back, and looks forward to expanding their donor base to include local corporations and professionals.

Rule 7: Make it verifiable. When you're using less traditional work, there is no "past employer" to vouch that you did what you say you did. So you must create a way for the employer to verify your proof. An article in the local paper that hails the reunion as a success and gives you credit can vouch for your skills in organizing the event. Your grandfather's doctor or visiting nurse could vouch for your skills with the elderly. Samples of your work could confirm your skill as a cook or website designer. A detailed but brief description (ninety seconds or less) of the rainy-day activities you designed with your kids can substantiate your creativity. Notes of thanks and praise from friends whose cars you fixed can attest to your mechanical skills. A list of "customers" you help (for free) could corroborate your skill. Or you could offer to do a work trial. If they can't verify it, most employers won't accept your word as proof.

Rule 8: Don't get pigeonholed by your past career. Use a skills résumé so you highlight your transferable skills, not your past jobs. (Remember, skills résumés are most effective with small to midsize companies.) Don't have all your Stories or Facts come from one job or industry that is different from the job you are now applying for. Be sure your Credible References market you for your new career, not your old job. And show more enthusiasm for your new career than for your old one.

Rule 9: Always prepare a good answer for the interview. Be ready to explain to employers why your skill is relevant to their business and to give the rest of the story about where you gained it. As you develop your answer, listen to it as if you were the employer, or ask a friend who is an employer to help you. We'll teach you how to do this in Chapter 16.

We've given you all the techniques and rules for using less traditional proof. Now let's put it all together. So how did Jason use his baseball coaching experience to prove he'd be a great assistant restaurant manager? First, he combined his previous restaurant experience with the leadership skills gained as a coach. Next, he made sure his transferable skills followed the rules—including using general business language instead of baseball terms. Here is an example of his proof using each of our four techniques.

1. Fact. *As the leader of a team of 14 people, I increased success by 60% within 8 weeks.* Rather than, *The team won only 1 out of 5 games the first half of the season, but won 4 out of 5 in the second half when I was coach.*

2. Demonstration. The clear and easy-to-follow connection Jason drew between being a successful coach and a great manager for the restaurant demonstrated his ability to take complicated or uncommon ideas and make them simple for staff to understand.

3. Credible References. A former employer vouched that he relied on Jason to run the kitchen when the lead cook didn't show up. Another verified that within seven months, she began pairing new waiters with Jason so he could train them.

4. Story. To prove his skills in problem-solving and staff support, Jason shared this Story: *One of my team members was ready to quit, so I took him aside for a chat. Turns out, he was unhappy about being transferred out of a position he felt he was good at. After evaluating the situation, I implemented a plan that allowed him to share the position, and sold him on using his strengths across two functions. This allowed me to retain his talent, and made him happy. In fact, he even recruited a strong new team member.*

Using proof from his coaching experience on his résumé and cover letter got Jason interviews. Sharing his proof in the interview impressed the employer, but it also raised a question: "Where did you get all this management experience?" When you use unpaid or less traditional experience to prove you can do the job, you *must* also have a good answer to explain it. Jason's good answer sounded something like this: *I've been successfully managing projects and teams for years—it's one of my natural skills and interests. To date, my management experience has been unpaid. The examples I've given you come from my work with a losing baseball team that I took to second in the league in the first year. I've been the manager for three years now. Sometimes, I think unpaid managers have an extra challenge, because the team they manage doesn't have the incentive of a paycheck to work hard or give their best. I'm really looking forward to using my natural skills and experience to make us both money.* Jason's proof and good answer resulted in two assistant management offers!

10

Proving You're the Person They Need

The historian Christopher Lasch observed that "nothing succeeds like the appearance of success." Your PADMAN Plan will help you highlight your success so the employer is impressed. We showed you how to use Facts, Demonstration, Credible References, and Stories, and now it's time for you to prove you're the person the employer needs.

MAKING PADMAN WORK FOR YOU

You know the job you want, and have listed your prospective employers' needs in each area of PADMAN. Now it's time to develop proof that you possess the attitudes, qualities, and skills they need. Let's get started.

Step 3. Prove You Can Do the Job

Review each employer need on your list, and ask yourself, *Why do I think I'd be good at this?* and *When have I done this before?* We often overlook our own strengths, so answering these questions with someone else who knows your accomplishments often produces greater results. Then, on the same line, under the column My Proof, denote which technique you intend to use to prove you can meet the need—Fact, Demonstration, Credible Reference, or Story. Write the details in a job search journal.

When writing the details in your job search journal, list the skill, quality, or attitude you've proven in a different color on the outer margin so it's easy to find. Remember, the same accomplishment can often prove several different skills or qualities. Keeping a journal may seem like extra work at first, but a couple of hours now will save you lots of time and frustration later. Once you've developed your proof, you can use it for lots of employers and adapt it for other jobs.

Employers value accomplishments from your paid work and formal education most, so look there first to prove you meet each employer need. Next, transfer proof from other fields, then less traditional sources, and be sure to follow the rules in Chapter 9. Tailor your proof to match the employer's needs. For example, if your knowledge or experience goes beyond what the employer needs, you may be screened out for being overqualified (employers fear you won't be happy with the level of salary or responsibility, willing to take orders from others, or stay long-term). Kick it down a notch—"seventeen years' experience" becomes "more than ten years'," "business owner" becomes "general manager," and an

SAMPLE PADMAN PLAN

	1. Job Target Office Assistant in a veterinary office	
	2. Employer Needs	**3. My Proof** Facts, Story, Demonstration, Credible Reference
P Presentation	• Casual professional image	☐ Facts ☐ Story ☑ Demo ☐ CR appearance/greeting
	• Good phone voice	☐ Facts ☐ Story ☑ Demo ☐ CR talk w/mgr on phone
	• Good handwriting	☐ Facts ☐ Story ☑ Demo ☐ CR handwritten thank-you
	• Energetic demeanor	☐ Facts ☐ Story ☐ Demo ☐ CR
A Ability	• Proficient in MS Suite	☑ Facts ☐ Story ☐ Demo ☐ CR 6 years experience
	• Know vet terms	☐ Facts ☐ Story ☐ Demo ☐ CR
	• Good with animals	☐ Facts ☑ Story ☐ Demo ☐ CR about lost dog in park
	• Customer service exp	☑ Facts ☐ Story ☐ Demo ☐ CR 4 years experience
D Dependability	• At work daily by 7:45 a.m.	☑ Facts ☐ Story ☐ Demo ☑ CR past employer
	• Organized so paperwork is accessible	☐ Facts ☑ Story ☐ Demo ☐ CR about reorganizing files
	• Complete tasks on time	☐ Facts ☐ Story ☐ Demo ☑ CR past employer
	• Honest/reliable with handling money	☐ Facts ☑ Story ☐ Demo ☑ CR trusted w/petty cash
M Motivation	• Task completer	☑ Facts ☐ Story ☐ Demo ☐ CR university deadlines
	• Loves animals but can handle seeing them put down	☐ Facts ☑ Story ☐ Demo ☑ CR my dog, my vet
	• Good team player	☐ Facts ☐ Story ☐ Demo ☑ CR Sally, coworker
	• Willing to do menial tasks	☐ Facts ☑ Story ☐ Demo ☐ CR volunteering at ASPCA
A Attitude	• Compassionate	☐ Facts ☐ Story ☑ Demo ☐ CR interaction w/pets
	• Emotionally strong	☐ Facts ☐ Story ☐ Demo ☑ CR My vet
	• Friendly	☐ Facts ☐ Story ☐ Demo ☐ CR
	• Willing to learn	☐ Facts ☑ Story ☐ Demo ☑ CR about vet terms in books and ASPCA vets
N Network	• Connections with local pet stores, trainers, and kennels	☑ Facts ☐ Story ☐ Demo ☐ CR can list 28 contacts
	• ASPCA volunteer	☐ Facts ☐ Story ☐ Demo ☑ CR ASPCA director
	•	☐ Facts ☐ Story ☐ Demo ☐ CR
	•	☐ Facts ☐ Story ☐ Demo ☐ CR

SAMPLE JOB SEARCH JOURNAL ENTRY

Presentation	Get hair trimmed, iron black slacks and striped blouse, shine shoes, wear stud earrings	Casual professional image
	Use good eye contact, warm smile, and firm handshake	Casual professional image
	Call office manager to confirm appt and demo phone voice	Good phone voice
	Drop off handwritten thank-you note next morning	Good handwriting
	Need proof—I'm shy with strangers	Energetic demeanor
Ability	Proficient in all Microsoft programs	Proficient w/ computer
	Tell Story about my recent hike in Fender Canyon, when a Labrador . . .	Not afraid of animals
	Animals are drawn to me	
	4 years' customer service between bookstore and ASPCA	Customer service experience
	Need to learn veterinary terminology and prove knowledge	
Dependability	Davy Zane, 913-555-0165	Reliability
	2/1—Called DZ, agreed to be a work reference & mention my dependability and accuracy on the register.	Honesty
	2/3—Sent thank-you note, w/ my key message and my résumé	
	Tell Story about fixing filing systems so files were no longer misplaced	Organized
	And about manager asking me to handle all petty cash	Honest
Motivation	In my 4 years at university, I never missed a deadline for a paper or project.	Task completer
	Need to call Dr. Flannery to make sure he's willing to verify the Fact, and get his email address	Meet deadlines
	Share Story about having to ask my vet to put Rover down	Strength to lovingly put down sick pet
	Ask vet to comment about me being good w/ animals	
	Ask Sally to be a personal reference. Ask her to include a story about me being a . . .	Good team player
	Ask ASPCA director to be a reference. Subtly remind her of my willingness to do what is needed	Willing to do menial work

"MA in Economics" becomes "course work in Economics," with no mention of your master's degree.

Once you've compiled your proof, notice how impressive you are. If there are a few employer needs you can't prove you meet, they become barriers you must overcome to get hired. In Part 3, we will show you how. For now, list any employer needs you can't prove you meet on the second page of the PADMAN Plan, next to the related PADMAN area under My Barriers. So if the employer requested *Good knowledge of the area*, you would write:

SAMPLE PADMAN PLAN

	4. MY BARRIERS
ABILITY	Lack knowledge of the area

If there are several key needs you can't meet, consider changing your job target to one your transferable skills match more closely. If there are only a few needs you can't meet, it shouldn't be a problem. If the thought of listing your barriers feels overwhelming, we understand. Don't be discouraged, you are in good company. Everyone has barriers to employment . . . even Bill Gates, the founder of Microsoft! He is a university dropout. Before he proved his worth, some employers would have screened him out. He has proven that neither age nor lack of education has to hold you back. In truth, many of the world's most successful people overcame major barriers on their way to the top.

Oprah Winfrey is an African-American woman in an industry dominated by white men. Today, she is one of the most powerful people in entertainment, showing that once you've proven your value, race and gender don't have to stop you from succeeding.

Tom Cruise battles with dyslexia, yet he and his directors have never let it stop him from learning his lines and creating blockbuster movies.

Chris Gardner, whose life story is told in the movie *The Pursuit of Happyness*, struggled through homelessness and single parenthood while proving to Dean Witter, a top financial company, that he was the best man for their highly sought-after stockbroker position. His persistence drove him to success, and today he is worth millions.

Each of these people faced barriers, believed those barriers could be overcome, and made it happen. Having barriers is not the problem, failing to deal with them is. In the next section we'll show you how to create solutions for your barriers, before they distract employers from seeing your true value.

PART 3

How to Avoid Being Screened Out

ong before employers decide which candidate is the best for the job, they focus on who to screen out, who else to screen out, and . . . who else to screen out. So no matter how brilliant you are, if you don't make the cut, the employer will never know it. We've taught you how to prove you can meet the employer's needs. Now we'll show you how to avoid getting screened out.

Screen outs are job and company specific, so removing them is not a one-time affair. It must be done whenever you pursue a new job. For example: Your lacking a driver's license will not concern an employer if he doesn't need you to drive and the company is located near reliable public transportation. However, if the company is in a remote location or may need you to run errands, it could be a screen out. Having changed fields several times may be perceived by one employer as well rounded and by another as uncommitted. And issues that are overlooked at a lower level may become barriers as you try to advance. Identifying what might concern a prospective employer about you for *this job* is the first step in eliminating or reducing the barrier.

There are two things that will get you screened out. First, you didn't prove you meet an employer need from their top ranked areas of PADMAN. (Remember, employers prioritize the six areas of PADMAN differently based on the job, company, and industry goals.) Employers are willing to do some training, but only if you prove you have the core of what they need. Core areas you can't meet will get you screened out unless you have a solution. Second, you'll be screened out if you didn't remove or minimize the unspoken issues that concern the employer. Even if they don't say it, most employers want employees who bathe regularly, won't steal or whine, don't swear at customers, or bring their personal problems to work, and the list goes on. Again, these distractions can come from all areas of PADMAN. If you don't remove them, a negative key message may develop— *He's the sweaty guy who talked too much and kept name-dropping* or *She's the one who kept complaining about her last boss and wouldn't look me in the eye.* To identify these problems, view yourself from the employer's perspective. Then create a solution, so the focus stays on your talents and you hear, "You're hired!"

The six solution tools we teach you in the next few chapters are simple, practical ways to honestly eliminate or reduce all the issues that concern employers. In twenty years of successfully helping people avoid getting screened out and land great jobs, we haven't encountered an issue that can't be overcome with these six tools (not to be confused with the six areas of PADMAN). Of course, they are not a magic wand that can change your age, create experience you don't have, remove a disability, or erase criminal history—but they don't have to. They only need to reduce the sense of *risk* employers feel, so their focus shifts to what they will *gain* by hiring you. The key to getting hired is to prove to employers that what they will gain *outweighs* any risks they are taking.

 ## THE 6 SOLUTION TOOLS

1. Learn a New Skill
2. Access a Resource
3. Change Your Job Target
4. Adjust Your Outlook
5. Adjust the Employer's Perception of You
6. Craft a Good Answer

There is no "one right way" to overcome your screen outs—you always have options. For example, if you lack the appropriate wardrobe, you might *access a resource* by borrowing or purchasing enough clothing for a week, while someone else might *change her job target* to match the clothing she currently has. In either case, the employer is never aware that there was a problem. That's the power of these six tools. When you use them correctly, barriers become nonissues. The only exceptions are barriers that employers will learn about when they interact with you or investigate your past. These require a *good answer*, and we'll teach you how to craft them so you reduce the employers' risk and highlight what they gain.

You will often combine tools to create your best solution. Anna's driver's license was revoked because of a DUI. She chose to adjust her *outlook* to embrace the idea of using public transportation, and *target* companies located near the bus route, where she could use side doors and résumés, instead of applications that would highlight her DUI. Finally, in case it came up in the interview, Anna crafted a good answer to explain why she couldn't drive (depending on the situation, she could simply say that she didn't have a license, didn't have a car, or was trying to be more "green"). Of course, if the employer asked a direct question about criminal convictions, she had to be honest, but even then her answer did not have to include the words "drunk," "alcohol," or "DUI." You'll learn more about carefully choosing the language for your good answers in the pages that follow. But for now, let's start with learning a new skill.

11

Solution Tool 1:
Learn a New Skill

→→ **A KEY TO SUCCESS**

In today's job market, lifelong learning is key to success, whether you're a high-level manager, a cleaner, or somewhere in between. To stay competitive, employers need people who are constantly learning and improving their skills. To be hired, you don't have to know it all now, but you must prove that you can learn what you don't know. You may need to gain a technical skill, like compiling profit-and-loss statements or driving a forklift, but technical skills are not enough. Employers also look for life skills (managing your time or finances), social skills (demonstrating good manners and hygiene), business culture skills (networking or business English), job search skills (explaining why you are a wise investment). Learning a new skill can help you avoid getting screened out, so you can prove you're worth hiring.

That the top 10 in-demand jobs for 2010 did not exist in 2004, that more unique information was generated in 2009 than in the previous five thousand years combined, and that for students starting a four-year technical degree now, half of what they learn in their first year will be out-of-date by their third year? It's all true, according to *Did You Know? 3.0: Globalization & the Information Age*, a video created by Karl Fisch and Scott McLeod.[1] Education is not about knowing everything, it's about learning how to learn so that when you graduate you can begin your education.

Some of the issues getting you screened out can be overcome by learning something new. The key is to determine *what* you need to learn, and *how* you can learn it best. Barb knows that to get promoted she'll need to get better at online research. Neil wants to learn to be a gardener. Errol doesn't know some of the latest software programs. Yoku wants to stay in America when she graduates and needs to learn Western business protocol.

If you enjoy taking classes and loved school the first time around, you can return. If you hated school, you'll be glad to know that learning a new skill doesn't have to happen in a classroom. Barb taught herself to research online by spending her evenings surfing the Net and reading articles on the subject. Neil targeted gardening services that offer on-the job training, because he enjoys learning by doing. Errol attended a weekend workshop to learn several software packages. Yoku observed how businesspeople interact on TV and in person, and then discussed her observations with her mentor, a college professor who is also a successful businesswoman. So Yoku would be perceived as professional, confident, interested, and honest, her mentor convinced her to get comfortable with the Western business greeting. Mastering the greeting is a simple way to counter what could otherwise tip the scales against you. This is particularly true if you're shy, from another country, young, inexperienced, pursuing work that requires a new level of professionalism, or have a physical trait that might cause others to dismiss you, such as being short or disabled. Try it, and note how others respond to you. Practice it until it is second nature.

☞ TAKING A PAGE FROM BUSINESS . . .

A simple greeting can create a positive, professional, and self-confident impression. In Western business culture, people greet one another by doing four simple, but essential, things:

1. Smile as they approach one another.
2. Maintain eye contact as they approach and while talking.
3. Offer a firm handshake.
4. Introduce themselves by name, or greet the other person by name if they've already met.

There are lots of ways to learn. Observation is often over-looked, but it's one of the easiest and most powerful. If you know someone who is good at something you want to learn, copy him! You could also attend college or university, either online or on campus. You can pursue a degree, or take a single class just for the knowledge. College has changed a lot in the last decade, and you may be pleasantly surprised at the practicality of many courses and the number of adult students. Even if you didn't attend college, had a bad experience, or it's been a while, consider it. Tour campuses online or in person and see what they offer. Another way to facilitate your own learning is by reading industry magazines and publications, listening to audio books or seminars, watching videos, or surfing the Internet. And we always recommend finding a mentor—a professor, successful professional, or someone who is more knowledgeable about or proficient at the skill than you—who can guide your learning. Not only can that person speed up your learning, she can also open doors for you.

DISCOVERING YOUR LEARNING STYLE

We all learn differently. One learning style is not better than another, but it helps to know your preferences so you can learn in the ways that are most effective for you. The three main types of learners, according to the popular neurolinguistic programming (NLP) therapy,[2] are:

Visual learners, who learn best by reading instructions, watching someone demonstrate the thing, and taking notes. If you enjoyed how teachers taught in school, this is probably your learning style. Continue learning by taking classes; reading books, magazines, and manuals; taking online or tele-courses, watching shows, reading blogs, or researching the topic online.

Auditory learners, who learn best by talking and debating with others, listening to verbal instructions, and asking questions. If this sounds like you, build relationships with experts you can talk to; join a discussion group or an online chat room or blog; attend workshops; listen to recordings; or watch shows on the topic.

Kinesthetic learners (also known as *do-ers*), who learn best by doing it for themselves and improving with each effort. If you like to get the basic details then "just try it" before getting too much more information, then this is your preferred style. Consider participating in on-the-job training, internships, or apprenticeships; attending hands-on workshops; watching and emulating a demonstration; or asking experts to show you how to do the task or review your trial and error.

Most of us are drawn to one of the learning styles, or a combination of two. Preferring one learning style doesn't mean you can't learn in other ways, just that you'll learn quicker and easier using your natural style. To learn more about the different learning styles and take a test to determine your learning style, visit www.the6reasons.com.[3]

CREATING SOLUTIONS BY LEARNING NEW SKILLS

Once you're clear on what you need to learn and how you learn best, just start learning. Once you've got the hang of something, continue learning from feedback given by experts—teachers, successful friends, employers, or mentors—and do it again! This is how it looked for Maureen as she learned how to impress a prospective employer at a lunch interview.

➡ DID YOU KNOW?

If the job entails taking customers out for a meal, it's common for employers to interview you over a meal to ensure your table manners reflect well on the company.

Hear It, See It, or Try It! Maureen applied for an account executive position that would require her to take customers out to eat. She was asked back for a second interview and was told it would be over lunch. Immediately, she browsed the bookstore for advice on business lunch etiquette: Use good table manners—don't talk with your mouth full, and keep your napkin in your lap and your elbows off the table. Avoid sandwiches or burgers with runny sauces, and anything that could get your hands dirty. Salad can make you appear health-conscious, but can get stuck in your teeth. Choose something you can cut into small pieces. Don't be too picky, demanding, or a complainer; the employer will think you're that way at work. Don't order alcohol, particularly if you are driving. And don't order dessert unless everyone else does. Remember, it's still business, so don't get too comfortable or too personal. Maureen realized that her lunch conduct would be critical to getting hired, so she called two successful friends who agreed to "interview" her over lunch the next day.

Just Do It! Preferably in front of someone who has enough expertise to give you constructive feedback on what you are doing right and what needs to be improved. Feedback from experts is the fastest way to learn. If you can't find anyone who is good at the skill, just do it on your own and review the results. If you don't like the results, make adjustments and try again. The sooner you start doing it, the sooner you'll learn the skill. Maureen arrived nine minutes early for the lunch "interview" with her friends. During the meal, she conducted herself as if she were in a real interview. She also paid close attention to what her friends did, and mirrored it. Once the meal was over, the feedback began. The outfit worked, but they suggested she put her keys, a credit card, some cash, and her lipstick in her briefcase and carry only one bag. Her greeting was perfect and her initial conversation was comfortable, but as the meal progressed she appeared too focused on "getting it over with." A business meal is about building relationships, so interacting in a humorous, casual nature is important.

Learn from the Feedback and Do It Again. Seldom do we master a new skill on the first try, so continue asking for feedback and making corrections until you get the results you want. Maureen practiced her lunch interview manners and casual banter at every meal over the next three days. In order to break any bad habits, she paid her son a quarter every time he caught her doing something wrong. The day before the interview, Maureen met one of her friends for breakfast and the other for coffee to demonstrate her developing skills and to get feedback. In the formal interview, Maureen was able to focus on demonstrating that she could impress customers and make sales. After the interview, she met with her friends to debrief. She planned to continue learning from what went right and what could have gone better. It paid off two interviews down the road. Today, she is a top account executive because she has never stopped learning.

A few more quick tips for overcoming barriers by learning new skills:

- If you have most of the qualifications for the job, ask employers about on-the-job learning opportunities for those you lack. Employers recognize that even excellent candidates may require some learning. Most offer some training for technical skills (ability) to ensure you do the job the way they want it done. Many are willing to develop staff in the other areas of PAD-MAN if they are asked and see clearly how it will benefit them. Demonstrate that you are eager to learn, dependable, and hardworking, so they believe you are worth the effort.
- If you are learning a new skill or have a plan to acquire it (for example, you have registered for a class or are meeting weekly with a mentor). Craft a good answer that highlights your desire to learn and explains your plan.
- If you aren't sure you want to learn the skill or you can't learn it before you need to start working, you can always change your job target using the ideas in Chapter 13. Once you have gained the required skill, you can reapply for the job you want.

- If you choose a field that fascinates you and work you truly enjoy, learning will be easier and more fun.

Learning a new skill is not just about increasing your *ability*. It can help you upgrade your *presentation*, portray the right *attitude*, demonstrate your *dependability*, show you have the *motivation* to make the company profitable, and help you cultivate a *network* that benefits the company. What could you learn—a new technical, life, social, business culture, or job search skill—that would help you avoid being screened out?

This is the first of the six solution tools you can use to avoid being screened out. Now let's look at what appears to be the most straightforward—accessing a resource.

12

Solution Tool 2:
Access a Resource

> **IF YOU DON'T ASK, YOU
> WON'T RECEIVE**
>
> Accessing a resource is often the simplest way to overcome a barrier, but it does require action on your part. Resources include *items*, like a computer with Internet access or professional tools, *services*, such as résumé writing or an image makeover, and *information*, like a list of colleges offering the training you need or employers looking for your skills, as well as *referrals* that allow you to access these resources. Finding and using resources can make your barriers disappear.

Sometimes, all that is stopping you from getting the job is a simple *item*. Howard's tools were stolen from his truck the night before he was to start a new carpentry job, so he called friends and family and borrowed what he needed to get started. Jeana was an excellent florist, but her dyslexia made it impossible to accurately write down phone numbers or addresses

SAMPLE
ITEMS JOB SEEKER MAY NEED

- Professional-grade tools
- Interview and work clothing
- Equipment or technology to accommodate a disability
- Access to a computer, the Internet, and a high-quality printer, scanner, or fax
- Bus pass or a vehicle
- Personal identification
- Professional briefcase or portfolio
- Image-creating jewelry
- Pay-as-you-go phone or personal voicemail box

when taking orders, so she purchased a simple handheld tape recorder to take down customer orders as she repeated them back. Often, accessing items can help you quickly create solutions and eliminate employer concerns.

Other times, you can overcome barriers by accessing a *service*. Some services are free, and others cost. To find the service you need, start with the Internet, a local library, the United Way, a Workforce Center, or your friends and family. TJ was a customer service agent in a framing shop who wanted to become a sales associate in an art gallery. He knew his image was getting him screened out, so, inspired by a television makeover show, he paid an image consultant to help him look the part. Maleeka's parents discovered a job coaching program for adults with mental disabilities that could work with her until she was proficient in her job as a grocery bagger. Often, utilizing the expertise of others can help you eliminate an employer's concerns so you can stay focused on proving your value.

Knowledge is power. Often, new *information* is the resource you need to overcome a barrier. Jess had always worked in manufacturing and didn't know what else he could do. At www .onetonline.com he discovered in-demand careers that use his skills, and decided to pursue one of the growing number of jobs as a refrigeration mechanic/installer. Georgette had used her criminology degree for less than a year before going overseas to work with an international aid organization. Upon returning to the United States a decade later, she realized she was seen as out-of-date. To change that perception, she visited the university library to read contemporary criminology textbooks and articles so she'd learn current industry vocabulary, as well as trends and happenings to discuss during interviews. Having new, useful information at your fingertips can help you remove your barriers, and give you added confidence as you market yourself.

SAMPLE
SERVICES JOB SEEKER MAY NEED

- Résumé writing
- Job search assistance
- Haircutting and styling
- Psychological counseling
- Negotiation training
- Dental work
- Speech coaching for an accent or an impediment
- Tattoo removal

Some resources are easy to access, but others require time and finances you may not have right now. Getting a *referral* from someone who can access the item, service, or information for you may be your best choice. Justine needed a car to get to the job site, but couldn't afford to get hers fixed. Her uncle talked with his mechanic, who agreed to fix the car and let Justine make payments. Russell needed experience, but even unpaid internships were hard to come by in the film industry. His sister's friend, a visual effects producer, referred him for a volunteer position building movie sets on an independent short film, which helped him establish his network and begin his career. Partnering with people who have access to the things you need will help you overcome barriers and shorten your job search.

CREATING SOLUTIONS BY ACCESSING RESOURCES

The process of creating solutions by accessing resources is pretty simple. Determine what you truly need, discover the best way to get the resource, and then access it. Your research can be as thorough or quick as you choose.

1. Determine what you truly need. If you don't identify the employer's actual concern, your solution won't work. Remember, their concern always comes back to profit. For Jeana, the florist mentioned earlier, the employer's concern was not her dyslexia but her ability to accurately record orders, because inaccurate orders decrease profit. If Jeana had seen her dyslexia as the barrier, she might have spent years trying to improve her condition before pursuing the job she loved. Accurately identifying the employer's concern allowed her to come up with a much simpler solution— using a tape recorder to insure orders were always accurate. Consider your prospective employer's *true* concern and determine the resource you need to eliminate that concern.

2. Discover the best way to get the resource. To quickly come up with lots of options, brainstorm with others about where to go. Often, the best source turns out to be the third or fourth idea you consider. When Howard, the carpenter above, had his tools stolen, his first thought was to call and quit before he even started the job. He considered getting the tools he needed by pawning some personal items, or explaining his bad luck to the employer and asking to borrow their tools, or requesting an advance on his pay. Luckily, he talked with friends and discovered

ADDITIONAL SOURCES FOR RESOURCES

- Former teachers and employers
- Local and federal government agencies
- Chambers of commerce
- Places of worship, charities, or community services
- Local service clubs
- Professional associations
- Staffing agencies
- Schools and universities
- Yellow pages or local resource guides
- Libraries

he could piece together enough tools to start his new job the next day. If you're embarrassed to approach friends, consider asking strangers or investigating online, like TJ did when he looked for an image consultant. When you investigate online, be sure to review consumer comments and ratings.

3. Access the resource. This may require you to ask for help. If that scares you, then don't ask for help, just ask for information, which sometimes turns into an offer of help. Using the telephone is a quick and easy way to investigate and access resources. Before making any calls, create a script and practice so you sound calm and get the information you want.

Once you have accessed the resource and resolved the barrier, employers don't need to know about it, because it is no longer a concern. However, there are three reasons you might choose to share your solution with employers:

- **If how you resolved the issue demonstrates a skill or quality the employer needs.** Russell could share how he got his start in the film industry through his networking ability and connection with a respected visual effects producer.
- **If your solution offers a resource the employer needs.** Maleeka's parents could explain how their daughter's job coach can save the company money in training.
- **If employers will become aware of the issue when they meet you, check your references, or watch you work.** In this case, you must prepare a good answer. Jeana knew that at some point employers would notice she had a problem reading and writing, so in addition to accessing the handheld recorder, she crafted a good answer that acknowledged the issue and shared her simple and creative solution.

Think of the reasons employers are screening you out. Which of your screen outs could be removed if you accessed an item, a service, new information, or a referral? Remember, with the right resource many barriers can be completely eliminated, so the employer never knows they existed.

Another great way to avoid getting screened out is to target jobs and employers for which your issues are not barriers. The next chapter will show you how.

13

Solution Tool 3: Change Your Job Target

Changing your job target is a quick way to eliminate barriers that hold you back. There are three reasons to change your job target:

1. You can't go back to what you did before. Perhaps the industry is diminishing, you've been injured and have limitations, you have a criminal conviction that disqualifies you, or you lack transportation, tools, or other necessary resources.

2. You don't want to go back to what you did before. Maybe it was too stressful, paid too little, required too much time away from your family, or you are no longer willing to conform to industry expectations. Maybe you've had an experience that makes the old job incompatible with your new values, such as having kids, discovering a new faith, getting clean and sober, or realizing that you don't have to endure abusive or unsafe working conditions.

3. You've identified a new direction you want to take. This is about looking toward the future or new goals, pursuing a field that fascinates you, using skills you enjoy, or accommodating a new lifestyle or value.

Knowing *why* you want to change your target will help you decide what to change and where to start looking. If you are changing because you can't or no longer want to use specific *skills*, consider other jobs in your current field that use skills or knowledge you already have and enjoy using. Randy was a pipe fitter for more than two decades before sustaining a back injury. He was sad to think he'd have to leave the industry he loved, until he realized he could use his extensive network and knowledge in commercial construction. He became an estimator. Randy also could have pursued sales for a construction supplier or equipment rental company, project or safety management, and even some driving jobs—none of which required him to use his bad back or leave the industry.

If you are changing your job target because you can't or no longer want to work in the *field*, consider jobs in other fields that use your current skills. Helen was tired of the constant travel required in medical sales, so she took her sales skills and her network of doctors to a new field. She became the membership manager for a golf course. A few other fields that would appreciate her sales skills, extensive network, and ease with high-end customers include fund-raising, real estate, and fine jewelry or art sales.

If you are changing your target because your current job doesn't match your *values* and you are unhappy, identify your most important values (making a difference, earning more money, feeling appreciated, time with family, and so on) and consider jobs in your field or skill group that support those values. Ted, a chef in a gourmet restaurant, recognized he was an alcoholic and joined AA. He wanted to continue cooking gourmet meals, but in a place that didn't serve alcohol. He chose a fitness resort/spa, but could also have targeted private hospitals, elite private schools, or companies that specialized in first class meals for airlines.

One common mistake people make when changing their job target is that they change everything. When changing your target, keep as much as you can . . . your proven skills, your knowledge of the field, or the positive attitude that comes with choosing a job that matches your values.

To explore the skills you want to use, consider the skills you most enjoyed using in past jobs, throughout your education, and in your personal life. Then think of other jobs that require them. Or visit O*Net at http://online.onetcenter.org, a partnership project with the Department of Labor, to discover other jobs that use those skills. Don't be put off by the acronyms and jargon, because the information is well worth it. O*Net gives information about thousands of jobs, including the required skills, education and training, pay range, and expected growth of the field. As you change your job target, choose jobs that rely on as many of your favorite skills as possible.

QUICK TIP FOR USING O*NET

Go to http://online.onetcenter.org. In the box labeled "Occupation Quick Search," type in a past job and you'll get a list of skills the job requires. If you know your skills, the "Advanced Search" will help you find jobs that utilize your skills, specific tools, and technology proficiencies. If you are transitioning from the military or from one field to another, go to "Crosswalks" and type in your military title or previous job to generate a list of civilian jobs that require the same skills. The "Find Occupations" tool indicates jobs that share similarities, as well as jobs that are "green" and "in demand." Tip: Most of the boxes that ask for a code also accept job titles written in plain English.

To discover your fields of fascination, consider what you enjoy talking about with friends, doing in your spare time, or learning about by reading, watching TV, or surfing the Net. If you choose broad fields like "people," think about what type of people fascinate you—children, seniors, professionals, disenfranchised, famous, and so forth. Reviewing the index or major headings in your local yellow pages can also point you to fields of interest, as well as hundreds of local companies and their phone numbers. If you want your work to focus on a specific field, community, or issue, look for related magazines, newsletters, or newspapers online or in print. Your local librarian, chamber of commerce, or associations can help.

To discover jobs that match what's important to you, list your most important values, then list every type of employer or specific companies that share your values, want people like you as customers, or are likely to be sympathetic toward those values. Dale had long hair he didn't want to cut, and visible tattoos he didn't want to cover. In many jobs, this would not be a problem, but Dale felt a corporate office offered him the best opportunity to use his skills and education and make good money. Even today, most corporate offices want a clean-cut look. So Dale brainstormed with friends and family about fields where his appearance would not be an issue, industries that targeted "people like him" as customers, and corporate offices where they had seen male employees with long hair or tattoos. His top three choices were entertainment, advertising, and Internet-based companies. Remember, as you narrow your focus and what you are willing to accept, you limit your opportunities. So know what is nonnegotiable for you, and realize that sometimes you may need to relocate or compromise to get your most important demands.

CREATING SOLUTIONS BY CHANGING YOUR JOB TARGET

A great way to discover jobs that combine your skills and fields of fascinations is to list the six skills you most enjoy using and three fields that fascinate you, then brainstorm with friends or colleagues about jobs in the fields that use the skills. Think outside the box because there are many more than come to mind at first. Don't be limited by jobs you've heard of or openings you've seen recently. Think of any jobs that capture much of what you want and give them a name—assisting movie stars, conducting research on the Internet, helping children, and so forth. For five minutes let the creative juices flow, and write down everything that comes up. Many of the jobs may seem very unusual, and that's okay. Chances are someone is getting paid to do them. Why not you?

➤ **DID YOU KNOW?**

The Dictionary of Occupational Titles[1] lists more than 12,000 distinct job titles. About 95 percent of us work in the 3,000 most common titles. The remaining 5 percent work in more than 9,000 unusual jobs, such as bridge painting, carpet designing, cow inseminating, personal shopping, artificial limb maker, and animal training for movies, just to name a few.

Afterward, eliminate any that don't interest you. Do some research to discover real titles and details about each job, then cross off any that don't match your values. Brian had been laid off from an auto plant. The skills he most enjoyed using were welding, assembling, problem solving, and, from his hobbies, SCUBA diving and snowboarding. His fields of fascinations were extreme sports, nature and being outdoors, and construction. Brainstorming with friends, he came up with a list of possible jobs, including equipment builder for extreme sports, leader of outdoor adventures for the public, and underwater welder for bridges, oil platforms, or shipping companies. Next, Brian did an online search to learn more about each job and compiled a list of potential companies he could call—for example, for underwater welder, he listed companies that offered training in welding underwater, made and sold welding equipment, and the Association of Diving Contractors, whose members hire welder-divers. A few investigative phone calls produced a good understanding of the transferable skills employers looked for, which skills they were willing to teach, and what he needed to do and learn before applying. Today, Brian is a welder-diver working on oil platforms around the world.

➤ **DID YOU KNOW?**

Employers who hire for uncommon jobs often provide on-the-job training because too few people pursue the jobs to justify dedicated college courses. Also, advertising uncommon jobs in the Open Market is often a waste of money because the general public doesn't understand the transferable skills required for them. If you're interested in one of the nine thousand plus unusual jobs, search in the Hidden Market. Prove you've got the basics skills and a desire to learn, then often the employer will hire and train you in the remaining skills!

A few words of caution about overcoming barriers by changing your job target:

- It may seem like there are no openings in your field of interest, but there are always openings. As people retire, move, quit, get promoted, and pass away, openings are constantly created. They may not be advertised to the public, so search in the Hidden Market. They may no longer be available in your area, so you may need to move. Don't ask yourself if there *are* jobs. Ask *whether* securing and maintaining employment in this field is worth the extra work it requires.
- Don't use your old résumé for the new job. Create a new one that tells employers why you are qualified for the job you want now. Use the skills résumé format, and be sure to use the terminology of the new industry to describe your transferable skills.
- If you are anxious at the thought of changing the field you work in, the skills you use, or the type of company you work for, you are not alone. Gather information

about new opportunities and talk with people who do the new jobs you are considering. Give yourself permission not to make the change if you don't like what you learn. Also, consider volunteering. It's a great way to try something new in a safe setting. Finding a mentor who can teach you the ropes and advise you along the way will offer you wisdom, support, and connections if you decide to make the transition.

- Finally, sometimes the problem is not the field or skills or values. Sometimes it's our outlook on the situation. Eric left his first job because his supervisor was "a demanding jerk." He left his next job because his boss was "a know-it-all." He decided to change his job target, and used his proven skills in a new field, only to discover that his new manager "had no idea how to lead or how to support him in his job." Do you see a recurring theme here? Eric could continue to change where he looks for work, but his inability to get along with people in authority is likely to make him hate every job he gets, and make each of his employers wish they hadn't hired him. If you find that the same problem recurs in every new job, perhaps it's time for some introspection and personal growth.

Knowing the job you want is important for a successful job search, but often what we *believe* matters just as much. The next solution tool helps you overcome barriers when it's your view of the situation that's getting you screened out. It also includes a description of the only attitude employers want to hire.

14

Solution Tool 4:
Adjust Your Outlook

> ⮞⮞⮞ **WHAT YOU BELIEVE MATTERS!**
>
> Sometimes it's the way you see an issue that causes the problem. Have you ever noticed how two people can face the same situation—getting fired, being discriminated against, or being convicted of a crime—and one becomes successful in spite of it, while the other becomes a victim of circumstance? Often, the difference is their outlook. What you believe matters, because it determines your actions and attitudes. Identifying and adjusting the outlooks that are holding you back can help you achieve your goals.

Why do some people seem to have all the luck—even when bad things happen to them they bounce back? It's usually because of their outlook. How we view the world determines how we handle the things life throws at us. That is why two people who experience the same situation can end up with different results. Take the example of two brothers who were abused by an alcoholic father. One became an abusive alcoholic, just like his father. The other was kind, sober, and successful, just the opposite of his father. When asked how they became who they are, both men answered, "Look at my father. How could I have become anything else?" Imagine two workers laid off when their jobs moved offshore. For one, it was a reason to give up control of his life and his hope for the future. For the other, it was an opportunity to start a new career. Both would say, "I was unexpectedly laid off. What else could I do?" Faced with the same situation, they experienced very different results. Their outlook made the difference.

Your outlook determines both your attitudes and actions, and it's often a combination of the two that gets you hired, or screened out. To understand the power of your outlook, think of it as a filter through which everything you experience in life passes. This filter determines how you react, because it colors how you see the world. If you have a clean filter, whether the water poured into it is clean or dirty the inevitable result is clean water. Conversely, it doesn't matter if you pour dirty or clean water into a dirty filter—you're going to get dirty water. So it's not what gets poured into the filter that determines what you get; it's the filter. A dirty mental filter is sometimes referred to as "stinkin' thinkin'," because it can pollute our lives, relationships, future opportunities, and happiness. If you don't like the results that your current outlook is producing, choose a new outlook that will produce new attitudes, actions, and results. Remember what Henry Ford said, "Whether you believe you can or believe you can't, you're right."

We're here to help you achieve your goals, so we refer to outlooks not as right or wrong, but as constructive or destructive in reaching your goals. If an outlook helps you attain your goal, it's constructive. If it hinders you from reaching your goal, it's destructive. To discover if your current outlook is constructive or destructive, evaluate if you are getting closer to attaining your goals, or if your efforts have stalled. If you're stalled, you may think *your* situation is different, and that you are justified in blaming your circumstances rather than your outlook for the results you are getting—as did the brother who became an abusive alcoholic and the laid-off worker who gave up. No matter what issue you face, it's likely that others have faced it and are now working and achieving their dreams. It can be done. The question is whether you are willing to adjust your outlook so it can happen for you.

Adopting a new outlook starts with self-examination. Begin noticing your outlook every time you don't get the results you want. Next, find someone who is getting the results you want, notice his outlook, and begin to emulate him. What attitudes does he project? What actions does he take? If you know someone like this personally, ask her what she says to herself when destructive outlooks creep in. Replace what you are saying to yourself with something that will help you get the results you want. *No one is hiring* may become *Good jobs will be filled today and I only need one.* And *No one is going to hire me once they realize . . .* can become *Other people with the same issue have overcome it, and I can, too.* Adopting a positive mantra can also help—*I'd be great at this job. I just need to prove it!* Memorize your key message and verbalize it to yourself often to reinforce why the employer would be lucky to get you. Make a list of your goals, or find an inspiring picture, and post it where you see it daily to stay focused on achieving your dream. Ask the person you are emulating, or another successful friend, to tell you when he sees you returning to your stinkin' thinkin'. Be accountable. It's key in changing old habits and maintaining new ones. Plus, we naturally become like the people we spend time with. Is the outlook of the people you spend time with constructive or destructive to your goals? If it's destructive, think of ways to spend more time with people who have a constructive outlook.

CREATING SOLUTIONS BY ADJUSTING YOUR OUTLOOK

In the job search, it is particularly important to have a positive and confident outlook. However, when we are unemployed or unhappily employed, it is easy to feel angry, afraid, or depressed. But that's the problem—most employers only hire people who appear positive and confident. To be hired, you must put aside any rightful anger, fear, or depression, and project a positive and confident outlook. Daniel Porot, a pioneer in the field of career design and job hunting,[1] teaches a concept he calls Job Beggar/ Resource Person. It highlights the differences between a resource person, who employers want to hire, and a job beggar, who they screen out. Over time, we have found it useful to divide job beggars into "depressed" and "desperate."

Let's consider the outlooks of all three so you understand how employers might view you, and decide if you want to make any adjustments. Depressed Job Beggars appear defeated, tired, discouraged, defensive, and entirely focused on themselves and their problems. This outlook is reflected in their presentation, body language, and voice tone. They haven't bothered researching the company, crafting good answers, or developing selling points to prove they meet the employer's needs, because they believe no one will hire them anyway. During an interview, if they get one, nothing about the work lights up their eyes, their answers are brief and poorly thought out, and they don't ask questions, so the interviewer feels like an interrogator. Employers sense that if hired, the person will require a lot of extra work.

Desperate Job Beggars appear the other extreme. Their outlook can be anxious and frantic, or angry and challenging, but always their desperation shows through. And, like all job beggars, they focus on themselves and their needs, rather than what they offer employers. Their desperation is evident in their presentation. They dress to show their importance—rather than dressing just one level up from the job (as we suggest). Their demeanor can be overwhelming as they try to take control of the interview, desperately attempting to convince the employer to hire them. Their answer to a single question can last several minutes, and they often jump from topic to topic, oblivious to the interviewer's disinterest. Their interviews are not conversations, but monologues. Their eyes light up and they get excited only about things that benefit them—compliments from the interviewer, or discussions about pay or job offers. Even their questions reflect their self-interest—*When will the hiring decision be made? What's the pay? Do you cover moving expenses? Are there opportunities for advancement or paid training?* Employers sense that if hired, this person may not work in the company's best interest.

Resource People appear positive and confident. They are calm and engaging, reflect the company image and personality, and focus not on themselves but on how they can contribute to the company's success. They greet the interviewer with a warm smile, good eye contact, and a firm handshake. They have done their research in order to prove they match the employer's needs in each area of PADMAN. They understand the employer's goals and how they can benefit the company. They have taken the time to craft good answers, determine which stories and examples best prove their point, and insure their actions match their words.

During the interview, they keep their answers brief and focused, knowing employers will ask if they want more information. They ask questions about the company's needs, not their own—*My résumé proves I have all the skills you've asked for, but I know to be great at any job it takes more. What makes someone great at this job?* Or *What record would I need to break to be a top salesperson within the first year?* Their questions are often designed to allow them to share an additional selling point. For example, *I noticed on your website that you are hoping to expand into ABC. Have you run into any difficulties in sourcing XYZ? . . . I have a couple of good contacts if you're interested.* Lastly, Resource People's eyes light up as they share their passion and enthusiasm for the field, the job, or the company. Employers view them as someone who can help solve problems and increase profit. They are seen as a person who has options, who will be hired by someone else if the employer doesn't grab them now.

➤ **DID YOU KNOW?**

The questions you ask, or don't ask, during an interview can be as insightful for the interviewer as your answers to their questions. Our suggestion is to always ask at least three questions during the interview. At least two-thirds must focus on issues that benefit the employer. Limit the questions that focus on issues that profit you, such as opportunities for advancement and benefits the company offers.

Which one sounds most like you? If you want to be a Resource Person but can't get past your depression or desperation, remember it's about perception. *Decisions are based not on what is true, but what is perceived to be true.* If you copy the actions and project the attitudes of a Resource Person, you'll be seen as a Resource Person. You may also be surprised at how quickly you attract other Resource People, and truly become one yourself.

If your outlook is getting you screened out, use these ideas to adjust it. However, it's not just your outlook that may require adjusting, sometimes it's the employer's. The next chapter offers a proven approach for adjusting the employer's perception of you.

15

Solution Tool 5: Adjust the Employer's Perception of You

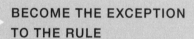

BECOME THE EXCEPTION TO THE RULE

Here's a difficult truth: Like other aspects of business, the hiring process is often not fair. Employers' concerns aren't limited to what's legal, accurate, or politically correct. Employers are human and, like all of us, make decisions based on their personal beliefs. So your age, gender, religion, disability, address, sexual preference, weight, ethnicity, and the like could get you screened out. Pretending it's not true doesn't change the reality. However, we have a simple, proven technique for changing the employer's perception of you: Demonstrate you're the exception to their belief.

Several years ago, Linda was negotiating with a successful businessman. When they finished, the man leaned back in his chair and said, "You're pretty smart for a blonde." The look on her face must have conveyed her shock at being the subject of the long-standing myth of the "dumb blonde." He quickly apologized. She smiled, and teasingly said, "I guess you haven't met many blondes." Her friendly challenge to his myth didn't necessarily make him believe that blondes are smart, but it politely pointed out that there are "exceptions to the rule," and it may have set the stage for him to notice other smart blondes that cross his path. Once he meets enough exceptions, he may be compelled to reconsider his bias and adjust his beliefs.

Let's further examine this idea that employer concerns may not be fair. When hiring, employers are especially sensitive about issues that have cost them money in the past, hurt a friend's business, or been highlighted in the news—even if they're not accurate, legal, or politically correct. This may seem unfair or shallow, but it's quite reasonable to base current decisions on past experience. We all do it. What feels unreasonable is how a few bad apples can spoil the reputation of an entire group. Most of us have heard comments like "kids today are irresponsible," "women are too emotional to make tough decisions," "people who don't have a job don't want to work," or "she's a dumb blonde." So what do you do when a stereotype, no matter how unfair or untrue, is threatening to impact your life? Pretending it doesn't happen leaves you unprepared to deal with it. Showing anger gets you labeled as someone with a chip on your shoulder. How do you persuade employers to look past their assumptions and see your value? The answer lies in adjusting employers' perception of you.

First some bad news: Persuasion is a slow and tedious process, because beliefs are deeply held, and intertwined with one another. Often, to change a single belief, a person must reconsider many beliefs. And the longer the person has held a belief, the more intertwined it is and the more difficult to change.

Now for the good news: We're going to teach you a shortcut. It's easier to convince employers that you are the "exception to their rule" than to convince them that their negative stereotype is wrong. Most people are willing to admit that there are exceptions to every rule. Presenting yourself as an exception (the one person for whom the stereotype is not true) can help you get the job. Later, you can help change the myth by introducing more and more exceptions, until the myth is no longer "the rule."

Notice that we use the word "myth" rather than "prejudice." We believe that much of what is termed prejudice is actually stereotypes handed down over generations without being challenged. They are based on ignorance, not malice (like the belief that hair color impacts intelligence). Once these stereotypes are challenged and evaluated by the person who holds them, they are often recognized as myths. Ignorant myths are easier to change than malicious prejudices. Clearly, malicious prejudice does exist, but the power of this approach is that when faced with a stereotype, you are better prepared mentally to present yourself as the exception, challenge the ignorant myth, and achieve your goal.

CREATING SOLUTIONS BY ADJUSTING THE EMPLOYER'S OUTLOOK

Here is how you can present yourself as the exception to the rule about negative myths employers may use to screen you out:

1. Stay focused on your goal. Work to be seen as an exception to the employer's negative stereotype, *not* to change her belief about "your group," whether that's high school dropouts, former executives, returning military, people with learning disabilities, ex-offenders, an ethnic group, or whatever. Changing those beliefs takes too long, and it usually starts an argument. David's story illustrates the point perfectly. David is a very capable, friendly administrative assistant who must deal with myths about people

> **BE A PERSON, NOT AN ISSUE!**
>
> No one hires older workers, single parents, the disabled, or career changers. They do, however, hire people they think can meet their needs who happen to be a part of one of those groups. Make yourself an individual, and focus on your value. As the employer gets to know you and listens to your good answers, she should decide that her initial concerns are not true about you, that she sees more value than expected, and that you are worth the risk.

with disabilities. Years ago, David lost an arm in a car accident. He has chosen not to allow others' stereotypes to frustrate him. In fact, he enjoys busting their myths and showing them what someone with a disability can do, as you'll see in his story that follows.

2. Remember that persuasion starts where they, the employers, are. So step into their shoes and honestly imagine the negative myths they may hold about "people like you," even if the myths are not true about you. You must also identify the potentially negative impact on profits those myths would have if they were true, because that is the employer's actual concern. These are the myths you have to bust. David knows from experience that people with disabilities are often perceived as helpless or needing others to do things for them, full of self-pity, sadness, or anger, and making people without disabilities feel uncomfortable. He knows that most employers will also be concerned about practical things like his ability to type, multitask, and carry things. Knowing this allows David to be deliberate about showing and telling them why none of it is true about him.

3. Once you understand the myth, determine the best way to prove you are the exception. This means showing or explaining how you are different. Most employers are not comfortable asking about these issues, even though they screen out for them if their concerns are not resolved. You have a couple of options. You can directly introduce the topic and explain how you are the exception, or you can subtly address the concerns without bringing up the issue. David chooses the first option. He has learned that the best way to deal with his disability is to confront it head-on, because he can't hide it. If he doesn't acknowledge it, employers politely interview him without asking about his disability, and without ever really considering him for the job. Early in interviews, David addresses his disability, often as part of his response to "Tell me about yourself." It sounds something like this: *As you can see, I have one arm, but this does not interfere with my ability to be a great administrative assistant. I can type 65 words per minute with my specialized keyboard, I use a headset to answer phones and free up my hand for other tasks, and my right arm is very strong, so I have no problem carrying and moving things. I actually think it's been a positive, because it's forced me to become very creative, and I often see solutions to problems that others miss.* (He is ready with a couple of stories that prove this point, if asked.) *Also, others often say that my positive attitude about my obvious disability creates a more positive can-do attitude among coworkers. I'm confident that when you talk to my references, they will say it has not been a disability.* Did you notice how David's good answer became about his abilities, not his disability?

Mo chose the second option—to subtly address the concerns without bringing up the issue. As an Arab-American Muslim, he knows that directly addressing negative stereotypes about race or religion could be seen as accusing the employer of illegal or prejudicial practices, and that's not how to win friends or influence employers. Laws have been designed to protect him against unfair discrimination, but he understands that it still occurs when employers believe the issue could cause a problem or cost them money. Mo is frustrated by the negative stereotypes, but he accepts that his goal is to get the job, not to change anyone's beliefs about *all* Arabs or Muslims. He'll present himself as an exception to negative stereotypes.

Mo recently graduated with a BA in Mechanical Engineering. He's confident in his ability and work ethic but knows he must address myths employers might have. As he and his friends list the myths, they note how, if it were true, each could negatively impact the company. Employers might believe that daily prayers and Muslim holidays would disrupt the work schedule, interfere with meeting deadlines, or cause staff problems if they're seen as special treatment. Coworkers and customers might fear that Mo is angry with America. Some employers might wonder if employing an Arab Muslim could disqualify the firm from government contracts. As Mo and his friends discuss these ideas, he has to fight his resentment, but at least he has a sense of the myths he needs to overcome.

Mo realizes interviewers won't mention these myths, so he'll need to find subtle ways to address them. He doesn't want to appear obsessed with the issue or introduce concerns employers don't have, so timing and tact will be important. To overcome concerns about cultural differences and his feelings toward America, he'll wear a business suit and be his positive, friendly, American self. He'll focus on what he has in common with the employer; he grew up in Wisconsin, went to school in the States, and holds season tickets for the Packers. He loves engineering and is excited about using his skills and creativity to do great things. He is hardworking, dedicated, and loves to learn. He is one of them.

Mo is applying to firms specializing in air quality and health care, so security clearance won't be an issue. He can discuss holidays and daily prayers with HR once he is offered the job. If these topics come up in the interview, Mo will reassure the employer that he will organize his schedule far in advance, and share a story about how his friend, an accountant with a large local company, has successfully handled daily prayers for years, including his willingness to simply pray in his heart when necessary.

If the interviewer feels comfortable, or bold, enough to ask about his culture, religion, or views on Muslim extremists, Mo will acknowledge their concerns and present himself as an exception: *With all that has happened, I understand your question. It makes me sad that many people have gotten a negative view of Islam. It teaches peace, self-control, charity, and kindness. This is what I strive for. My faith is a personal matter and I will minimize its impact on work. My goal is to be an excellent and reliable engineer for you, and a credit to my faith and my country—America. If this doesn't address your concerns, I am happy to answer additional questions.*

Whether you choose to be direct or subtle, remember, actions speak louder than words, so make sure your actions and attitudes back up what you say! In the end, employers must feel that although their myth may be true about some people, it's not true about you. This allows them to look past the myth and focus on your value as an individual.

◎ **THINK ABOUT IT . . .**

The hiring process necessitates discrimination. Employers must discriminate between the skills, experience, and the fit of everyone competing for the same job. After all, only one will be hired.

---

4. Once you are hired, be a raging success at your job! Keep a positive attitude, and continue to prove you are the exception to the rule, because the myth can easily be reasserted.

If you don't want to become the exception to the rule, you don't have to. Some people find the challenge exciting and purposeful, but others find it lonely and frustrating. If you don't have a strong desire or the fortitude to be a pioneer, simply *change your job target*. David could have approached companies under contract to employ people with disabilities, or that had already hired "people like him." He chose to focus on the job he wanted and adjust the employer's perception about him. Mo could have chosen to approach companies owned by Muslims or that do business in the Middle East. Instead, he, too, chose to prove he is an exception, with the hope of changing the rule.

If you want to actively work to change the employer's stereotype, once you are hired, begin introducing other exceptions and keep doing so until the rule no longer applies. This may take years, but it is possible. History is full of examples: In the United States, at the beginning of the twentieth century, it was generally believed that black athletes were not strong and agile enough to compete with white athletes. In the 1950s, it was commonly believed that women couldn't sell large-ticket items like real estate, stocks, and cars because they had no money sense. In the 1970s, it was believed that no one under the age of fifty had the wisdom to run a Fortune 500 company. Before the rise of YouTube and shows like *American Idol*, it was believed that the only way to become a famous musician was to first sign with a major record label. These myths have been well and truly busted. So if you want to be a myth buster, prove with your actions that the myth about your group isn't true.

We just showed you how to craft a good answer to overcome employer bias. Now it's time to learn how to craft good answers for other barriers that may be used to screen you out.

16

Solution Tool 6:
Craft a Good Answer

NOT ALL ANSWERS ARE *GOOD* ANSWERS

This is particularly true when it comes to addressing barriers. A *good* answer minimizes employers' *concerns* while offering proof that you meet their *needs.* It tells employers why the risk they are taking in hiring you is outweighed by what they will gain. Side doors or a strong résumé can get you an interview, but your good answers get you hired! You need to craft a good answer for every issue that employers may discover during the hiring process—most other barriers will have been resolved by one of the five tools described already. If you don't, you're giving the employer a reason to screen you out. Our proven process allows you to honestly answer even the toughest questions.

ood answers are your chance to convince the employer you're the right person for the job. As with all sales, what you say and how you say it often determines if the customer "buys." We taught you how to effectively address issues of employer bias in the last chapter. Now we'll show you how to craft good answers for the three other issues that often get job seekers screened out:

1. Nontraditional employment choices
2. Situations in your personal life
3. Patterns or mistakes in your past

Our approach reduces employers' concern without giving the issue undue importance, and it redirects the employer's focus to what they gain by hiring you.

 WHAT ARE EMPLOYERS AFRAID OF?

It is important to understand the employers' concerns. Here are a few reasons applicants are screened out, and what employers tell us they suspect:

- **Left a Good Job Without Securing Another Job.** Was compelled to leave due to an issue that might also negatively affect my company.
- **Changing Fields.** Lack specific knowledge, transferable skills, and expertise needed in the new industry. Isn't committed to the new industry and won't stay.
- **Long Stint of Unemployment.** Doesn't like working, has poor work habits or outdated skills and knowledge, will quit and return to previous activity, or other employers have noticed something wrong that the interviewer hasn't yet discovered.
- **Reentering After Retirement.** Skills and knowledge are not

CRAFTING GOOD ANSWERS FOR
NONTRADITIONAL EMPLOYMENT CHOICES

Nontraditional employment choices include things like leaving a good job before you have another job, returning to work after a long period of unemployment, or pursuing jobs for which you are overqualified. These realities require good answers because employers need reassurance that your reason for making the choice will not negatively affect their business. In fact, to be hired, you must prove that your reason will benefit the company. For example, if you are overqualified, employers worry that you only want the job because

current. Applicant is not used to the pace and expectations of work, lacks stamina, won't fit in, or won't stay.

- **Parent Returning to Work.** Focused on home not work, child care issues, outdated skills and network, won't stay.
- **Woman in a Trade.** Won't be accepted by male coworkers, won't stay, or won't have the physical strength and stamina for the job.
- **Male as Child Caretaker.** Not empathetic enough, too rough, will make parents uncomfortable, or there will be accusations or concerns of abuse.
- **Underqualified.** Can't do the job well or at all, will require too much time and training to be effective, or lacks the commitment and follow-through needed to learn.
- **Foreign Work Experience/Degree.** Can't communicate effectively, doesn't understand the business culture or have the same work ethic, or isn't familiar with the ideas, methods, and tools taught in this country's universities.
- **Advance Degree with No Experience in the Field.** Expects top dollar without offering any evidence of ability to apply the knowledge, or loves learning rather than working.

you can't find one at your level, and once hired you'll quickly become dissatisfied with your lowly position, be difficult to manage, discover you are rusty at hands-on tasks, want to move up immediately, or leave as soon as you find a better job. Or they may wonder if you are moving down the career ladder because of a problem that could cost them a lot of money, like gambling, stealing, not keeping your skills current, or being unable to get along with superiors. However, employers love to get top skills for less money! To get hired, you must give them a reasonable explanation about why you are happy to use your talent in a lower-level job, and convince them you'll stay.

Other nontraditional employment choices that may need explaining include changing fields, being underqualified, getting an advanced degree without gaining any actual experience, or choosing a job for which people of your gender, age, religion, or other group traditionally don't apply.

To craft your good answer, first think like an employer. Consider why your choice might concern her, how it could negatively impact her business, and how it actually benefits the company. Also, remember that employers don't have all the information you do, so think about what they actually know or see. Joe recently left a good job because he hated his boss, but the interviewer only knew he'd left a good job. When asked about it, Joe didn't mention his dislike for the boss. He stayed positive and shared a couple things he enjoyed about the job (the team, opportunities he had to learn or achieve), then he attributed his leaving to something positive (a desire to change fields, increase responsibility, learn something new) and explained how this next step in his career would benefit his new employer. He addressed the interviewer's concern, not the question, allowing him to reduce the concern without telling on himself. Look at your nontraditional employment choices through the employer's eyes, then use these three steps to reduce her concerns and focus her on what she will gain by hiring you:

1. Acknowledge the employer's concern in a positive way.
If the employer asks about it, acknowledge the issue, but put a positive spin on it. Rather than saying, *It's true. I am overqualified*, say, *I know I have worked at a more senior level, but . . .* or *It's true. I'm a woman applying for a job usually done by a man* becomes a lighthearted *I enjoy being one of the guys, even if I am the only woman.* This positive beginning is the first step in taking the edge off the issue. Keep your body language relaxed and engaged. Maintain a pleasant facial expression and good eye contact. When appropriate, include a touch of humor in your eyes.

2. Minimize the employer's concern. Briefly explain why the employer's concerns are not true about you. You can do this by giving a reasonable alternative explanation, or by sharing the steps you have taken to insure your choice will not negatively impact the employer's business. Don't use generalities. Instead, offer specific proof. And don't lie. It will come back to haunt you. An overqualified person might say, *I know I have worked at a more senior level, but I promised myself that one day, when the opportunity arose, I would work in this field. When I heard about this job, I felt the time had come. I know it is at a lower level than my previous job, but that means I can successfully do this job while learning the ins and outs of the new industry. And I look forward to a long and successful career with the company, just as I had with my previous employer.*

👍 QUICK TIP

Keep your good answers focused and brief, thirty to sixty seconds total. Saying too much can make you look desperate. If they want more information, they will ask.

---

3. Tell employers what they gain. End your good answer by sharing what the employer will gain by your nontraditional choice, and by hiring you. Include your top selling points for the job and a unique quality, skill, or attitude you offer that few other candidates bring. Your goal here is to insure employers feel that what they gain in hiring you outweighs any risks they are taking.

Here are some sample good answers for nontraditional choices, along with step numbers to make them easy to dissect. Note how they are crafted, then develop good answers that are true for you.

Reentering After Retirement: (1) *A few years ago, I retired early to spend time with my family.* (2) *If I had known then how much I'd miss working, I never would have done it. I enjoy the thrill of solving problems and making things work. I got involved with some community projects that were rewarding, but the truth is I want more. I've stayed current on the industry through the Internet, news, and a couple of colleagues, and* (3) *I'm in the process of reconnecting and expanding my professional network, which confirmed within me that I want to spend the next five to ten years lending my knowledge and skills to help a midsize company like yours compete with the big boys.*

Long Stint of Unemployment: (1) *It's been a while since I've been paid for full-time work,* (2) *but I have stayed busy and used the time well. After being laid off, I realized I'd be more valuable if I broadened my skills, so I began a combination of self-study and course work focused on . . . As I investigated jobs that use my skills in and outside my field,* (3) *I discovered that my ability to . . . is what's needed in this job. And in this day and age when everything changes so fast, my newfound appreciation for keeping my skills cutting-edge can benefit us both.*

Woman in a Trade: (1) *I enjoy being one of the guys, even if I am the only woman.* (2) *I guess that comes from growing up with three brothers and all their friends. I knew how to tear apart and* *rebuild a truck engine before I learned to drive. My dad always said my small hands gave me an advantage, because I could reach into tight spaces more easily. And I am stronger than you might think, so I have no problem using that advantage. I know some guys don't think women belong under the hood, but my skill and sense of humor won them over in the army and I know it will do the same here. (3) Besides, it always looks good to have an integrated shop when going for lucrative government contracts.*

Changing Fields: (1) *I'm fortunate to have had a successful career in the XYZ field, (2) and after more than ten years, I'm ready for a new challenge. With the downturn in my previous industry, now seemed like the right time to make the move. I've always had a fascination with ABC. In fact, I read several daily blogs and newspapers, including . . . which is how I discovered this opportunity. Also, I'm involved with several related community projects. On one, I . . . (3) I discovered that many of the skills and qualities that made me successful in XYZ are also valuable in ABC. For example . . . Most important, my contacts and understanding of how things are done in XYZ will give us an advantage in ABC because . . .*

Parent Returning to Work: (1) *It's been a while since I was paid for full-time work, (2) but I assure you I have not been idle. I have spent the last several years improving my multitasking skills by raising three smart kids who are all in school now. I've loved spending time with my children, but I'm actually very excited about getting back to work. I keep my knowledge current by reading ABC industry magazine and have stayed connected with many friends in the field. That's how I learned about this position. My family is very supportive, and I've organized great child care for the kids when they are out of school. And it will be a good thing for them to see that I, too, have "homework" many nights. (3) In addition to my skills and knowledge, I think you will find that my excitement and energy are two of my greatest strengths.*

CRAFTING GOOD ANSWERS FOR SITUATIONS
IN YOUR PERSONAL LIFE

Most employers know from experience that personal problems can translate into problems on the job. So issues you think are none of their business become their business. Chances are you'd feel the same way if you were interviewing someone to take care of something you value, like your child or your home. Employers may be sympathetic to your struggles, but they can't allow it to hurt their business. Remember, they're in business to make a profit, not create jobs. So keep your personal and professional lives separate—even after you're hired.

If your personal problems come up in the interview, you must explain why they won't impact your ability to be a great employee. Some personal issues that could get you screened could include: not having a plan to provide care for children or sick relatives who depend on you, living far from the workplace or not having a car, planning to get pregnant in the next few years, being currently embroiled in any legal action, such as a messy divorce, having a physical limitation or medical condition, having a bad credit history, or being new to the area. Employers are more likely to ask about some of these issues than others, so prepare the good answers you might need, and hope you won't have to use them.

Again, start by thinking like an employer. Considering why the issue concerns employers, and how it could negatively impact their business, will reveal the specific concerns you must eliminate. Use these three steps to keep your answers short, sweet, and solution-focused:

1. Welcome the question or acknowledge the concern.

This is important because it shows that you are up front, confident, honest, and concerned about the employer's business, rather than defensive and problematic. If the employer asks a direct question, stay relaxed, look him in the eye, keep a pleasant facial expression, and welcome the question with something like, *I'm glad you asked, because I wanted the opportunity to share . . .* or *It's personal, but if I were you, I would want to know, too, so . . .* Spend only two or three seconds welcoming the question. If the employer doesn't ask, but you believe he will be concerned when he discovers the personal problem later in the interview or during a background check, it's advisable to proactively acknowledge it yourself—for example, *You may have noticed . . .* or *I wanted to let you know . . .* Caution: If you know the employer is aware of the issue but he seems unconcerned about it, say nothing or subtly address it as Mo did in Chapter 15. Directly mentioning it could make the employer wonder if it's worse than he thought, if you don't maintain personal boundaries and will be talking about it at work, or if you have a chip on your shoulder about it.

2. Share your solution. Briefly share the steps you have taken to insure the issue will not be a problem for this employer. Don't just say it won't be a problem; spend five to fifteen seconds giving the employer specific proof. As you will see in the samples that follow, this statement does not need to be long, just specific. Too much information can give the issue too much importance or inadvertently cause you to tell on yourself. The employer can always follow up if he has additional concerns.

3. Tell employers what they gain. Complete your good answer by tipping the scales back in your favor. Remind the employer of what he gains by hiring you. You may even be able to turn lemons into lemonade by showing how the barrier is actually a selling point. Caution: When turning lemons into lemonade, be sure the selling point is something the employer values that is hard to find. Otherwise, your efforts might leave a bad taste in his mouth. Here are several sample good answers about personal issues. Again, don't copy them exactly, but use the three steps to craft answers that reflect what is true for you.

Child Care: (1) *I'm glad you asked. I am happy to share my plan.* (2) *I've arranged for child care with a center that picks the kids up from school and keeps them as late as seven o'clock. Plus, I have a neighbor who stays home and has agreed to watch them when I work late or if they are sick and my folks aren't available.* (3) *If anything, being a mom has made me an expert at multitasking and planning ahead, which will be a valuable skill in this job.*

Transportation: (1) *It's true that I don't have my own car, but the nice thing about* (2) *using public transportation is that I can organize my day, catch up on my reading, and not worry about breaking down, finding parking, or fighting traffic.* (3) *Besides, I'll get to work twenty minutes early. You'll find that I'm a person who likes to give the extra.*

Overweight Appearance: (1) *I am sure you have noticed that I am a very large woman. I know that initially it can make some people uncomfortable,* (2) *but I find that my friendliness and openness helps others get comfortable quickly. Being on your team means I'll interact with customers on the phone, so it won't be an issue, and I am sure my positive attitude can win over your team,* (3) *just as it will win over your customers. I am really good at this job, and can make both of us a lot of money if given the chance.*

Legal Problem: (1) *There is a personal issue I think you have the right to know about. In fact, you may have already heard about it.* (2) *I'm currently involved in legal action with XYZ Company. I'm a manager, so I understand this may cause concern, and I welcome the chance to address it. I've never been involved in a lawsuit* *before. I see legal action as a last resort, not a starting point, and I never would have taken action if the company had just refunded my money when I asked. Instead, they told me that if I wanted it back, I would have to sue for it, and that the court backlog worked in their favor. I'm a reasonable and patient person, but I know where to draw the line. (3) In fact, that's part of what makes me a great manager, along with my ability to inspire people to always do better than they thought they could.*

There are some personal issues you can wait to discuss until after you've been offered the job, but before you sign the contract, such as a disability accommodation, a medical condition the company should know about in case of an accident (hemophilia or AIDS), or a physical limitation that could affect health and safety on the job, such as poor hearing for a machine operator. It's best to talk with an HR representative about these issues because they understand the company's obligations and resources, and can communicate with the right people. At this point it's extremely unlikely the company would rescind their offer, because none of these issues stop you from doing the job. Waiting to mention the issue until after you're hired could cause employers to feel deceived.

 QUICK TIP

If you want to request time off for a previously scheduled commitment—vacation, appointment, or family event—ask after they offer you the job, but before you say yes. This ensures it's not used against you in the screen-out process while making it part of your negotiations increases your chance of getting a yes. However, know that the company has the right to say no to your request.

CRAFTING GOOD ANSWERS FOR MISTAKES
IN YOUR PAST

Employers assume if you've done it before, you'll do it again—steal, quit, harass coworkers, or make the company a million dollars! If there is a dramatic onetime *event* or concerning *pattern* in your past that employers wouldn't want you to repeat, craft a good answer that explains why it won't happen again. Do this even if you think the issue won't come up, wasn't your fault, or isn't legal for them to ask about. Dramatic events include a criminal conviction, having been fired, and suing an employer. Concerning patterns include repeatedly resigning without another job, relocating, quitting to return to school, and being laid off. The key word here is *repeatedly*. One time is understandable, repeatedly is a pattern. It's perfectly legal for employers to ask about these patterns, so if they discover them, they probably will. Plus, if they're interviewing you, they're already interested, so it's worth explaining.

Before you craft your good answer, examine the issue by asking yourself:

- **What caused it to occur?** If it was an action you took, why wouldn't you do it again in a similar situation today? If you would do it again today, skip this section because our process won't work for you. If it was something that happened to you, even through no fault of your own, consider if there were things you could have done to avoid it—not to assign blame, but to see if you have some control over whether it happens again.

- **How big a problem was it? When did it last occur? Is there a pattern?** It's easier to explain if it happened only once, was a long time ago, or had only a minor impact on a past employer or your life.
- **Why did it stop? Why would you not do it again, or why won't it recur?** Your answers to these questions are essential to reducing the employer's concern.
- **What has changed in your life that would make an employer believe it's no longer an issue, or won't recur?** What steps are you taking, or have you taken, to ensure the issue doesn't recur or negatively impact future employers, especially on this job? What proof can you offer?

With these details in mind, step into the employers' shoes and consider when they will learn about the issue and what questions they might ask. It's your job to use this information to craft an honest answer that reduces their concern and proves you are worth giving a chance. You will use five steps to craft good answers for these issues, and each step is critical. If you skip one, the good answer won't work. Let's take a quick look at the process, then we'll give you several examples.

1. Welcome the question. Let's face it. When these issues arise, the employer's concern is at the front of her mind and you've got some explaining to do. This can be an awkward spot in the interview for both of you. In that moment, lots of job seekers get defensive, resentful, or just try to avoid the issue. Their body language, eye contact, facial expressions, and energy make the whole situation worse. Don't let this be you. Don't waste time wishing the issue wouldn't come up or getting angry if it does, just be prepared. Craft a good answer, and start by welcoming the question. This two- to five-second investment sets a positive tone for the rest of your good answer.

2. Take responsibility for your actions and choices. If you don't take responsibility for your part in the mistake or problem, employers believe you are powerless to stop it from happening again, which makes you a big risk! Howard said it wasn't his fault he was fired; he was provoked by a bully everyone hated. Letty said she was unfairly let go; other people were taking things, too. Lisa said she couldn't help the fact that she was laid off from her last three jobs; it's the economy. There may be some truth in what they say, but they are less likely to get hired if the employer has other qualified candidates.

To take responsibility, determine what you could have done differently to stop the problem from occurring. Howard could have walked away and let HR deal with the bully. Letty could have refused when others suggested she steal. Lisa could have worked to make herself more valuable to the company or chosen a more stable industry. Briefly explain what happened and why. Don't blame others, deny your role, or dwell on your mistakes, and don't brag, smile, or make light of the situation. If you can do it honestly, attribute it to something you have already changed, like the wrong crowd, being young and stupid, or a bad decision you would not make today. Keep it short, five to fifteen seconds, so you don't get into gory or distasteful details. Also, avoid using *scary words*.

Another important part of crafting this sort of good answer is to carefully choose how you refer to the past. Which sounds farther in the past, "in 2002" or "almost nine years ago"? For people over thirty, the "almost nine years ago" sounds farther back. If you want something to seem farther in the past (like being fired, entering the field, or immigrating to the country), state the number of years ago it occurred. If you want to make

WATCH YOUR LANGUAGE!

"Scary words" are anything that employers are not expecting to hear in your interview that startles them so much that they stop listening to the rest of your explanation. They become stuck at the scary word, and never hear how you have changed, where you're at today, and why you're great for the job. Here are some alternate words you might use, not to deceive employers, but to tell the truth in a less startling way so they hear your entire good answer before deciding if the gains outweigh the risks.

Fired: Contract ended; mutual termination; agreed I should leave

Quit: Chose to pursue other options or opportunities

Laid Off: Company downsized; elimination of department; company relocation

Harassment: Behaved badly; acted inappropriately

Mental Illness: Resolved or managed medical condition; chemical imbalance

Chronic Illness: Resolved or managed medical condition; successful medical procedure

Inmate: Resident; contact with the criminal justice system

Burglary: Went into a building I had no business being in; took some things

Assault and Battery: Harmed someone; physical altercation or disagreement

Drug Addict: Resolved medical condition; substance use

Alcoholic: Drank too much; social drinking that got out of hand

High School Dropout: Left school early; entered the workforce early

something sound more recent (like a course you took or an article you wrote), use the year.

3. Share your moment of clarity. At this point, you have taken responsibility for your actions, but that is not enough to convince an employer you won't do it again. And simply saying you've changed or learned your lesson won't convince him either. You must let the employer see inside your heart and head. You must share your moment of clarity—the specific instance when you realized your mistake, regretted your action, and determined to change. It must give the employer a clear reason to believe you wouldn't do it again. Bob, who was fired for embezzlement, said, *It was the horror and sadness in my son's eyes when he found out that broke my heart. I knew none of it was worth it.*

The drama of your moment of clarity must match the weight of the issue. More serious issues require more dramatic moments of clarity to persuade the employer you have really changed. For lesser issues, your moment should be less dramatic, but still include the specific lesson you learned and your motivation for doing things differently in the future. Monica, who had been fired for being late, said, *I'll never forget the shock I felt when she fired me right in front of my coworkers. I assumed that if I did a good job while I was there, I couldn't get fired for being late. Man, was I wrong!*

As you decide how to express your moment of clarity, think about what the employer values. Does your explanation make it sound as if you're only sorry you got caught and are finding it hard to get a job, or that you regret the problems you caused others, as well as yourself? Keep it brief, five to ten seconds.

4. Paint a new picture. Now it's time to bring the employer from the past to the present. Paint a picture of your life today. Share what you have done or are doing to insure the mistake will not recur. Perhaps you have changed your thinking, become a parent, finally grown up, have a new group of friends or a new faith, learned a new skill, or caught a new vision for your life. Take fifteen to twenty seconds to help the employer see that where you are today is very different than your past. Every change you mention must be demonstrated in your actions and attitudes throughout the job search, and once you are hired.

5. Tell employers what they gain. The first four steps reduce the employer's concern in just thirty to forty-five seconds. In this final step, you redirect the employer's focus away from the risks and toward what she will gain if she gives you a second chance. You want to end your good answer by reminding the employer why she should hire you. What unique qualities, skills, or attitudes make you worth the risk? Be sure the employer feels like she can follow up with clarifying questions. For example, Bob, the man fired for embezzling, should expect employers to ask how much he took, over what period of time, how he got away with it for so long, and how he paid it back. What follow-up questions might an employer ask you? Prepare and practice your responses before the interview.

Here are several sample good answers for past mistakes, including the step number so you can easily dissect them and develop answers that are true for you:

Bob was fired for embezzlement. (1) *I'm embarrassed to have to tell you this, but you have a right to know.* (2) *It happened several years back, after my son was accepted to an Ivy League school and the tuition was more than I could afford. I thought the easiest answer was to give myself a small loan from the company. I was such a fool. Once you start taking shortcuts and lying to yourself, it just snowballs. In some ways, I was relieved when I got caught,* (3) *but it was the horror and sadness in my son's eyes when he found out that broke my heart. I knew none of it was worth it.* (4) *I wish we had just sold our home, gotten a smaller place, and paid for his schooling in the right* *way. I know I will spend many years proving to everyone, including you if you hire me, that I'm worthy of a second chance. I've made amends to my former employer and paid every penny back. I've also worked very hard to earn my family's forgiveness. I know firsthand the cost of taking shortcut, and will never make that mistake again. Hiring someone with a past is a risk, but I know my determination to be worthy of a second chance makes me worth it. I'm not asking you to trust me with your money, (5) just to let me use my education and experience with complex contracts to insure you maximize your profits. When I took over the XYZ contract for ABC company, I was able to reduce their expenses and increase profits by . . .* (Bob couldn't expect to be trusted with access to funds, so he targeted positions that require his advanced math skills to conduct complex statistical and costing analysis.)*

Jeff was terminated for fighting on the job. (1) *Thanks for asking. I wanted a chance to explain. (2) I loved that job, and I'm sorry I let it slip through my fingers. I was on a great team. Most of us got along really well, but there was one guy who was a real bully. He took credit for other people's ideas, stole sales, was inappropriate with female staff, and bullied people into keeping quiet. One day, I saw him corner a new girl, about the age of my daughter, and I stepped in and told him to back off. He shoved me, and without thinking, I reacted. The company had a policy that any physical altercation resulted in termination, so we were both let go. Soon after, on the recommendation of that boss, I started my current job. (3) At first, I didn't think I'd done anything wrong, but one day a friend told me how he would have handled it. The moment he said it, I knew he was right. He would have made his presence known without getting within arm's reach, and the bully would have had to back off. He couldn't do anything with witnesses around. Then he would have walked with the employee to HR, where they could both have reported it. (4) These days, I still look out for the little guy, but*

I use the chain of command. This incident was over three years ago, and nothing like it has happened since. I'm not a hothead, (5) *but I am a very good at ABC with a proven track record for XYZ, which can benefit your company by . . .*

Lisa has been laid off from her last three jobs. (1) *I'm not surprised you ask. It's been an interesting ride.* (2) *For the last twelve years, I have been a manager in manufacturing, and loved it. But as you know, companies are struggling to maintain profits. Two of my last four employers offshored their manufacturing, and the company I worked for most recently found it impossible to maintain a competitive edge and a decent profit in the increasingly global market, so they had to close their doors. The first two times my job was eliminated, I considered leaving manufacturing, but chose to stay because I enjoy it so much. Perhaps I should have made the move sooner.* (3) *At a recent change management seminar, I met several managers who work in the ABC field and it sounded interesting. I realized my talents could be of use here, and I could get off this roller coaster.* (4) *After the seminar, I did some field research to determine my best fit, joined a regional industry association, and began a course in . . . to gain more industry-specific knowledge. I really enjoy it!* (5) *I am confident that my twelve years of managing diverse teams and exceeding targets, and my drive to excel in this new field will make me an asset to your team. In fact, my last employer said . . .*

Corey had a pattern of quitting jobs after working less than a year. (1) *I'm glad you asked, because I wanted to explain.* (2) *The truth is, I was never big on long-term planning. I have always done what interested me, and moved on when I got bored. I thought that doing an excellent job while I was there was all that mattered.* (3) *It wasn't until I was talking with a friend who owns a business that I realized how much it costs a company to replace me when I leave—not just the time and cost of recruiting and training someone new, but also getting customers comfortable with a new rep,*

WHAT'S LEGAL, WHAT'S NOT

We are often asked what employers can legally ask about and consider when hiring. In the United States, the broad answer is: anything that they can prove affects your ability to do the job or impacts the safety of others. This includes experience, education, certificates and licenses, health and ability, criminal convictions, age (under forty), transportation, workers' compensation claims, lawsuits, credit history, and more.

It's illegal for employers to consider gender, race, color, national origin, religion, age (over forty), disability, marital status, sexual orientation, or pregnancy. Some employers perceive that these issues have a potentially negative impact on their business. While most are careful not to ask about them when hiring, others are ignorant of the law and don't realize they are over the line when they do, and some employers know the law, ignore it, and use these issues to screen out anyway.

If interviewers can get you to volunteer information that is illegal to ask about, they remain within the law. The question, "This is a demanding job. Do you have your family's full support?" can result in you revealing details about your marital status, sexuality, number and ages of your children, ties to the community, and other details. We heard of an employer who complains of a sore back during interviews, and casually asks candidates if they know of a good chiropractor, prompting them to give details about their health and fitness. An interviewer may apologize for being late and express the woes of managing child care to see if you join in.

Unfortunately, reminding employers that a question is illegal or refusing to answer it usually results in a shortened interview and no job offer. This is why it's so important to prepare good answers before you start interviewing, so you have a plan for presenting yourself as an asset who will benefit their company. Chapter 18 will more offer more help. For more information about what is and isn't legal in hiring, visit www.eeoc.gov.

especially when they really liked me. I've worked for great companies, and never would have hurt them if I had known. (4) So I've decided it's time to choose a challenging job in a field that fascinates me so I have challenges that stretch me. I know I'll want to develop my career within your company (5) and make us both happy I stayed. As discussed, my past successes prove I am very good at . . .

TIPS FOR MAKING YOUR GOOD ANSWERS MOST EFFECTIVE

- **Be Honest.** Developing good answers is not about fooling the employer long enough to get the job, but about helping him understand and see beyond issues that could distract him from hiring you. Don't lie just to get hired—you'll both be sorry.
- **Consider Your Audience.** Good answers only work if the employer listens and accepts them. Consider which employers are most likely to listen to your story, see beyond the issue, and hire you. It may have to do with their gender or age, or the industry or company culture. Watch each interviewer's eyes as you deliver your good answers to see if he remains interested or is screening you out. Use the ideas in Chapter 18 to tip the scales back in your favor, or at least to choose a more sympathetic employer next time.
- **Know the Question.** Before the interview, think about how the employer might ask about the issue, or how you want to start the conversation. Will he ask a direct question, or an open-ended question hoping you divulge the information? If you're going to bring the issue up, first tip the scales in your favor by

establishing your value. Once the employer is aware of the benefits of hiring you, give your good answer. Also, practice discussing follow-up questions in case they come up.

· **Make It Natural.** Use your own words, as long as they're not *scary*. Practice each good answer until it feels and sounds like you, fits with your overall presentation, and is a natural response to questions on the subject. *Natural* is beyond *memorized*, so practice delivering your good answers in the mirror and making sure your facial expressions match what you are saying.

· **Don't Give Up.** Realize that not every employer will be sympathetic to your issue, or willing to give you a second chance. It's a numbers game. Expect to share your good answer a half dozen times before you get a yes. Don't give up after the first interview. Watch the employer's reaction to your good answers. If he appears to stop listening, note exactly what you are saying when you lose him, so you can improve your answers.

Our twenty years of experience have proven that investing time in crafting good answers will increase your confidence and shorten your job search! We've taught you our six solution tools for minimizing or eliminating any barrier. Let's return to your PADMAN Plan and overcome yours.

17

Overcoming Your Barriers

You've just learned our six techniques for overcoming all barriers. As we stated from the beginning, they're not magic wands, but with your creativity and effort they can produce miracles. We've discovered that the only barriers that can't be solved are those that you don't take the time to address, or are unwilling to address. In our book *No One Is Unemployable*,[1] we offer further support to this claim by sharing sample solutions for eighty-eight common barriers. Scrutinizing your PADMAN from the employer's perspective will help you find your barriers so you can fix them before employers notice them. So let's get started on the final steps in your PADMAN Plan.

MAKING PADMAN WORK FOR YOU

You have discovered how to complete the first three steps—Step 1: Choose your job target, Step 2: List the employer's needs for each area of PADMAN, and Step 3: Prove you can do the job—now it's time to identify and remove the barriers that are getting you screened out.

Step 4: Identify Your Barriers

At the end of Step 3, you transferred any employer needs you could not prove you met to the My Barriers column on your PADMAN Plan. These are employers' spoken concerns. Now it's time to add the unspoken concerns you think they may have. Review yourself in each area of PADMAN for anything that could distract employers from hiring you, even if they haven't asked for it, such as bad teeth for face-to-face customer service jobs, a depressed or desperate attitude, your age if you're older or younger than those they usually hire, being a single parent of young children if your job requires dependable attendance, changing fields, and so on. Here are four ways to catch additional barriers before the employer does, so you can remove or minimize his concerns:

- Ask for honest feedback from friends and relatives. Often, others know us better than we know ourselves. It may be difficult to hear, but it's valuable.
- Ask an employment specialist who spends her days looking at candidates through the employer's eyes so she can make a good job match.

SAMPLE PADMAN PLAN	4. MyBarriers	5. Solution Tools Learn a New Skill * Access a Resource * Change Your Job Target * Adjust Your Outlook * Adjust the Employer's Perception * Craft a Good Answer
P Presentation	• Poor eye contact (spoken need— energetic demeanor)	☑Skill ☐Resource ☐Target ☐Outlook ☐Perception ☐GA ☐Skill ☐Resource ☐Target ☐Outlook ☐Perception ☐GA
A Ability	• Don't know vet terms (spoken need)	☑Skill ☐Resource ☐Target ☐Outlook ☐Perception ☐GA ☐Skill ☐Resource ☐Target ☐Outlook ☐Perception ☐GA
D Dependability	• No childcare plan (unspoken need)	☐Skill ☑Resource ☐Target ☐Outlook ☐Perception ☐GA ☐Skill ☐Resource ☐Target ☐Outlook ☐Perception ☐GA
M Motivation	• Haven't done research in the past (unspoked need)	☐Skill ☐Resource ☐Target ☑Outlook ☐Perception ☐GA ☐Skill ☐Resource ☐Target ☐Outlook ☐Perception ☐GA
A Attitude	• Shy with strangers (spoken need— energetic demeanor)	☑Skill ☐Resource ☐Target ☐Outlook ☐Perception ☑GA ☐Skill ☐Resource ☐Target ☐Outlook ☐Perception ☐GA
N Network	• From rough part of town (possible unspoken need)	☐Skill ☐Resource ☐Target ☐Outlook ☑Perception ☐GA ☐Skill ☐Resource ☐Target ☐Outlook ☐Perception ☐GA

- Review the list of common screen outs at www.worknet-international.com and honestly consider if each could be perceived as true about you.
- Evaluate your job search results. If you're not getting interviews, not getting offers, have had people decline to act as your reference, evaluate why.

Once you've listed your barriers, notice which area of PADMAN has the most and which has the least. This will show your areas of strength and weakness. Also notice how your areas of strength and weakness stack up against the employer's top priorities for PADMAN.

Step 5: Create Your Solutions

Now that you know what's getting you screened out, create your solutions! There's always more than one way to minimize a barrier, and we've given you six proven tools—access a resource, learn a new skill, change your job target, adjust your outlook, adjust the employer's perception of you, and craft a good answer. Which you choose depends on what will satisfy the employer, and on your preferences. Imagine you discover your current image is getting you screened out. *If you think it's reasonable*, you might adjust your outlook and gather the resources so you reflect the company's image while at work. *If you think it's ridiculous*, you could target companies that value your current image, or craft an answer to convince employers you're the "exception to the rule" and can still make them a profit. *If you resent it to the point of rebellion*, you could start your own company, or you could decide not to change anything and take your chances.

To choose the best solution tool for each of your barriers, ask yourself:

> Which tools can eliminate the barrier so the employer will never know it existed?

> Of those tools, which do I want to use?

> If I change my target, which employers wouldn't consider this issue a barrier?

SAMPLE JOB SEARCH JOURNAL ENTRY

Presentation	Poor eye contact	Practice good business greeting with a smile and maintaining good eye contact
	Shy with strangers	Remind myself that I don't have to feel friendly & outgoing, I just have to make the customer feel welcome and cared about
Ability	Don't know veterinary terms	Visit university bookstore to review veterinarian terms from textbook glossary and practice them with staff at ASPCA
Dependability	No childcare plan	Talk w/ Mom & Alice about helping when baby is sick and can't go to day care
Motivation	Haven't done research in the past	Adjust outlook to view research as a means of getting hired and promoted, not busywork
		Then get online, talk to my vet, and develop questions to ask the various vet offices I'll be applying to
Attitude	Friendly	Choose several warm and friendly greetings I can offer new customers
		Practice saying hi first and do it with a smile and good eye contact
		Share with employer that I know it's important to make new customers feel valued and welcome
Network	From a rough part of town	Subtly demonstrate in words and actions that I won't bring my neighborhood culture into the office

If employers could become aware of the barrier even after you have applied the tools, craft a good answer. On your PADMAN Plan, under Solution Tools, review each barrier and indicate the tool(s) you will use to overcome it. Note the who, what, or how.

In your job search journal use what we've taught you to detail how you will overcome each barrier, and write out your good answers. At www.worknet-international.com, you'll find a free Mini Solutions Bank with tips for avoiding over fifty common screen outs. Prioritize your barriers. Start by resolving the issues that stop you from job searching effectively—job target, child care, or company image. Then, tackle the issues that reduce your job search success—demonstrating a new attitude from the one that got you fired, crafting good answers, or looking for side doors. You can address barriers that stop you from getting promoted once you're hired.

You know your employer's needs and have created proof that you can meet them. You've identified and removed the barriers that could get you screened out. Now you're ready to create an effective job search strategy.

PART 4

Creating an Effective Job Search Strategy

t is true today and will ever be true that the person who is hired is not necessarily the one who is best qualified for the job, but the one who knows the most about how to get hired," according to Richard Bolles,[1] international authority on job hunting. Our final advice will help you tip the scales in your favor, target the right employers, and pull together everything we've taught you into an effective job search strategy. Your strategy should include how you'll divide your time between the Open and Hidden Market, whether you'll focus on using the front door or make the effort to find side doors, and which approach—paper, phone, walk-in, or Internet—is best for you when contacting employers. Each can highlight or minimize both your barriers and strengths, so be deliberate when creating your strategy.

Let's take a final look at how to tip the scales in your favor.

18

Tipping the Scales in Your Favor

Throughout the job search process, everything you say and do is placed on scales in the employer's mind—the *costs and risks* of hiring you on one side, the *benefits and gains* on the other. The employer makes a wise investment when the benefits he gains outweigh the risks and costs. So the candidate who offers the most gains and least risks at a good price gets hired. That's why it's essential to offer all of your related accomplishments, including those transferred from unpaid and less traditional sources (just follow our rules). You must also transform your general selling points into proof that what the employer *gains* significantly offsets your barriers. Mr. Matthews illustrates this point well with a story about a candidate he once hired for his warehouse. He was interviewing for temporary warehouse workers, a forklift driver, and an assistant manager. Larry applied for the forklift job, but was willing to start as a temp worker to prove his value.

Larry arrived ten minutes early and was neatly dressed in work boots, nice jeans, an ironed, button-down shirt, and a tie. He was obviously fit and seemed friendly. Larry had the required license, more than ten years' experience, was willing to take whatever shifts were available, and seemed eager to work. When Mr. Matthews asked Larry what he thought were the major problems companies faced with warehouse staff, he was impressed with Larry's answer—damaged merchandise, theft, carelessness, and not getting the job done. Larry then proceeded to share why these would not be problems with him. Mr. Matthews wasn't surprised to learn that Larry had been a supervisor in a previous job. At this point, the scales were tipping in Larry's favor. Near the end of the interview, Mr. Matthews was startled by Larry's admission that he had a criminal conviction for drug sales. The scales just tipped in the other direction! If Larry started using or selling drugs, the four major problems they discussed earlier could all occur.

You might be wondering why Larry "told on himself." He knew his conviction would be discovered when the company did a background check, and he didn't want it to screen him out. By telling Mr. Matthews himself, he had the opportunity to tip the scales back in his favor. He told Mr. Matthews that it was important to him to be honest, and that he didn't want them to discover it later and feel like he had misled them. He was hoping to stay a long time with the company. He assured Mr. Matthews that he hadn't used or sold drugs for three years, and offered to take regular drug tests. He also explained the government bonding program that offers extra insurance as a safeguard to employers who give good people a second chance. Mr. Matthews watched Larry's eyes as he spoke, and his gut told him Larry was one of those good people. But there were still several more candidates to interview.

➤ **DID YOU KNOW?**

Employers commonly believe that a job seeker's eyes show honesty and dishonesty . . . as well as their passion for the job.

Sensing that Mr. Matthews was not convinced, Larry asked if his concern was because the company had problems with drug use in the past. Mr. Matthews admitted they had. Larry responded that he could help. His experience meant he could easily identify who was using and encourage them to clean up. He even knew of a free recovery program they could take advantage of. Also, he could help create a clean shop, where those who use drugs feel pressure not to bring it to work. Larry's up-front style and earnest responses impressed Mr. Matthews. He no longer saw Larry as a potential problem, but as part of the solution, and the scales tipped back in his favor. Because of Larry's good answer, positive references, supervisory experience, and his own gut feeling about him, Mr. Matthews offered him the assistant manager position.

Over the years, we've been surprised at what people tell potential employers. We once worked with a man who wanted to start interviews with, *I'm Nate, a grateful recovering addict.* We said, "Good answer, wrong meeting!" He'd never been convicted of a crime or lost a job because of his former drug use, so there was no reason to bring it up. He said he didn't want to lie. We agree that you should *never lie to an employer.* It will come back to haunt you, often resulting in getting fired and a bad reference. However, there is a difference between a lie and appropriate disclosure. If an employer directly asks about an issue, offer an honest good answer using the techniques in Chapter 16. But few interviewers will ask if you're a single parent, upside down in your mortgage, attending therapy, going through a divorce, chronically ill, or if

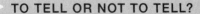

TO TELL OR NOT TO TELL?

There are a lot of things about you employers don't have the right to know—for instance, that you struggle with depression, are planning to have a child, are in recovery from an addiction, or your sexual orientation or marital status. But there are two reasons why you might choose to tell them:

First, like Larry, you may *know* the employer will discover the issue when she does a background check, talks to your references, or at some other point in the hiring process, such as with issues like having been fired, a criminal conviction, pending legal problems, the revoking of a related license, a medical problem that interferes with regular attendance, and so on. It is true that many small companies hire on intuition and won't investigate your past, but many of them do conduct background checks before offering promotions. If you suspect that the employer will discover the issue, offer your explanation before he hears about it from others. However, bring it up only after he is impressed and shows an interest in hiring you, so you have lots on the gain side of the scale before adding potential risks to the other side.

Second, there may be an issue that is important enough to you that it must be supported in your work environment, such as having your sexuality respected, being able to talk about your faith, or taking calls from your kids. Again, wait until the employer sees your value before bringing it up, but discussing it during the interview allows you to see the employer's reaction and decide whether the company is a good match for you.

Most interviews are only thirty to sixty minutes long, which is not much time to share all the reasons you would be an asset to the company. Don't misuse that time by focusing on the risks.

you drink too much . . . unless you give them a reason to be con-cerned. Appropriate disclosure means *not volunteering negative information the employer will never discover that doesn't affect your ability to do the job*. If an issue has been resolved, say nothing!

If you are unsure whether your references or a background check will reveal the issue, do a check yourself. Helena discovered that her past employer never mentioned her sexual harassment law-suit. Walt discovered that his employer simply said the contract had ended, not that he'd been fired. CJ discovered that his criminal record was sealed because he was a minor when he committed the offense. Ask an employment advisor or friend to conduct a refer-ence check on you. Have her call the HR Department or manager at your previous companies and state that she is doing a reference check for (your name and social security number) who reportedly worked for their company between (your dates of employment) as a (your position). Once your associate verifies those facts, have your friend ask the company rep if he would recommend you for (the job you are now pursuing). If the rep is talkative, your friend can ask about some of the accomplishments listed on your résumé to see if the company confirms your claims. Have her end the conver-sation by asking why you left and if you are eligible for rehire, and if you aren't eligible, why. It's important to get the facts.

➤ **DID YOU KNOW?**

Most HR Departments will only verify the starting and ending dates of employment, position, and salary of former employ-ees, and whether they are eligible for rehire. Often, smaller and independently owned companies will even give details about the quality of work and reasons for leaving. Due to increasing lawsuits, a growing number of employers will only verify basic details in writing with your signed consent.

Another thing that can tip the scales against you is casual comments you make without thinking. Rina mentions that she recently visited Disney World and looks forward to going back once she and her husband have kids. The employer wonders how soon she wants kids, how long they will be paying for her maternity leave, and if she'll come back. Garth says that his wife doesn't want to move, so he will be commuting almost two hours each way to the job. The employer worries that the extra hours will get old quickly and Garth will be gone. Bonnie shares that she worked in the field for seven years before she got married, and now needs a job because her #§*#^ soon-to-be ex won't pay a reasonable alimony. The employer imagines her on the phone with her lawyers, rather than his customers. None of these issues had to come up. Step into the employer's shoes and review your recent interviews. Have you shared information that tipped the scales against you? Often you can see it in the employer's eyes. Here are some tips for handling three common questions:

Tell me about yourself. Keep your Stories and Facts focused on skills, qualities, and attitudes the employer is looking for. Don't bring up personal information that doesn't add to your image of being great at the job—being native to the area could illustrate stability, where being a single parent of three could do the opposite. As you prepare your response to this question, consider each item you want to include and ask yourself whether the employer needs to know this, and if it will prove you would be great at this job. Your best answer to this question will use Stories that highlight your key message.

What is your greatest weakness? Carefully choose the weakness you will share. Choose a skill or quality you are currently working on that is related but not essential for the job—*I am more comfortable working with customers over the phone than in person, which is why I'm applying for a back-of-the-house position.*

But I really want to get better at face-to-face interaction so I joined Toastmasters and have begun to volunteer at Chamber of Commerce events. If you had said, *I can't swim,* the interviewer would likely have thought, *What does that have to do with anything?* Also, avoid overused "weaknesses," like being a workaholic or perfectionist. Employers don't believe them, and you seem sly using them. If you have an *obvious* weakness in an area the employer needs, sharing it and your solution demonstrates honesty and a desire for professional development. Be sure also to remind the employer of what you offer that counters the weakness—*I currently type 35 words per minute, but I'm taking a typing class and have already increased my speed by 10 words per minute. Within 3 months, I should be over 65 words per minute. I am hoping that my experience with . . . more than makes up for a slightly slower start.*

Why would you be great for this job? With humble confidence, share your key message, including your unique hard-to-find quality, attitude, or skill. Keep it brief, and end by sharing your best Story regarding your key message. *For more than 10 years I have been successful managing programs like yours. I have an excellent network throughout the United States, which can increase our visibility; it was built in part by service on the board of ABC Industry Association. And most important, I share your passion for helping people. I know managers and senior staff in our industry can become jaded, but I find that our clients inspire me. In fact, just last week I encountered a young mother who attended a college program I managed. Her newfound success and confidence is why I do this job.*

TARGETING THE RIGHT EMPLOYERS

In every field there is a wide range of employers, and what they're looking for varies. That's why PADMAN is so valuable.

Identify employers who need what you offer, and match what you want. If you are a paralegal, would you get a better reception from legal aid or a corporate firm? If you want to be in retail sales, is Macy's or the Dollar Store a better match? A colleague was surprised when an interviewer commented that her purse was quite expensive and perhaps that nonprofit agency wasn't the right place for her. Target employers who value your unique selling points and will be attracted to your personality and image.

Consider your barriers, and which employers are more sympathetic or inclined to give you a second chance—it's often based on their age, gender, ethnicity, socioeconomic level, or industry. For example, we heard of a tailor with severe facial burns who found that storefront tailor shops and department stores were uncomfortable with his appearance, but employers in the medical and protective services were more sympathetic and luckily had a lot of uniforms that required tailoring. A woman who had successfully sued a previous employer for sexual harassment found that professional white men in their thirties and forties were more accepting of her explanation than female and older interviewers (perhaps because they were raised in an era of heightened sensitivity to gender issues). What's your issue? Who should you avoid? Who is likely to understand your situation, listen to your good answer, look beyond the issue, see your worth, and take the risk? Target them. If you're not sure, take note of the reactions you get from employers and track who's sympathetic and who's not.

19

Choosing the Strategy That's Best for You

Every job search tool, market, and door has its upside and downside. They can highlight or minimize your strengths as well as your barriers. So choose carefully. Don't leave your job search to chance. Deliberately plan your strategy.

Having an effective strategy is key to every business endeavor. In most companies, 80 percent of income comes from 20 percent of customers, so to stay in business they pay special attention to that 20 percent. This 80/20 rule[1] also applies in a job search. You'll be more successful if you focus extra effort on a few select employers than if you give moderate effort to many. Look in the Hidden and Open Market to select a handful of companies to focus on. Create a PADMAN Plan for each and find a side door that puts you in front of the person who has the power to hire. Job searching in the Hidden Market will give you access to more than 85 percent of available jobs, including unusual jobs that are seldom found in the Open Market. It allows you to target companies that interest you, rather than settling for what's offered to the general public, and it lets you demonstrate, as you search, the qualities and skills the employer is looking for. The downside to the Hidden Market is that accessing it requires research, creative thinking, and the confidence to do something different.

In the Open Market, you know where the jobs are, but so do hundreds of other people. However, if you use a side door, you can avoid being part of the clamoring horde of job seekers waiting at the front door to be screened out. The only time we advise using the front door is if you're staying in the field, have a stable work history that shows upward progression or technical development, offer impressive accomplishments, and have Credible References. In this case, create a PADMAN Plan for the job, and then tailor it for each ad you answer. Use a chronological résumé, register with employment agencies or headhunters that charge the employer rather than you, and scour the Internet, newspapers, and industry publications for job postings. In all other cases, we recommend using side doors.

Side doors allow you to approach decision makers before submitting your résumé or application, or asking for a job. By their very nature, side doors are unique; although we shared a dozen examples earlier, we can't give you a step-by-step process for them. Side doors are designed to help you stand out. If everyone started using the exact same side door, employers would either add better security (as they've done with cold calls over the phone) or start treating it like a front door, complete with traditional screen-out protocol. What we can give you are the four keys needed to open side doors, and examples from successful job seekers. The keys are simple, but all four must be used to open a side door.

1. Get noticed for the right reason. You can't do what everyone else is doing and expect to get noticed. Be creative, but don't get noticed for the wrong reasons. *Stand out from the crowd by offering a hard-to-find quality, attitude, or skill that the employer wants!* We have shared dozens of examples. Here's another creative approach that worked. A young man camped outside the headquarters of an oil company in cold weather, stating he wouldn't leave until he was considered for a position. This side door demonstrated his ability to endure hardship, which is valuable when working on oil rigs, and his commitment. Several days later, a rep from the oil company said if he was that determined to work for them they would consider him. Of course, if a hundred people had camped out on the company lawn, a visit from the police would have been more likely than a visit from a hiring manager. And if the man had camped out in front of a law firm, the police surely would have been called because this side door doesn't emphasize qualities a law firm would value.

2. Get noticed by the right person. Demonstrate your hard-to-find quality, attitude, or skill in front of the person with the power to hire, or someone that person trusts who could be a Credible Reference for you. Only these people can allow you to bypass the screen-out process and get on the short list. Mandy wanted a position in the deli of a large grocery store. They were using online applications to screen people out, but she knew the final decision would be made by the deli manager. So she went in as a customer, asked to see the deli manager, and complimented him on the quality of their products. She began coming in once or twice a week, on the days she knew he worked. She always made a small purchase, and casually said hi. Once, they briefly discussed her love of cooking, and another time she shared how she had "sold" a neighbor on one of the deli's specialties. After several weeks of demonstrating her friendly personality and love for the store, she mentioned to the manager that she was thinking of going back to work and couldn't think of any place she'd rather spend her time. She then asked how she could get a job in his department. He asked a few questions, then explained that she must submit an online application, but that he would contact HR.

3. Don't ask for a job or submit a résumé until after you've impressed the decision maker. If you do this too soon, your résumé will be added to the mix with everyone else's. If Mandy had merely submitted her application, it could easily have been screened out before she got an interview. Had she told the deli manager on their first meeting that she was looking for a job, she would have been reduced from valued customer to "job beggar." Impress the employer before you talk about employment. If you give it time, employers will often say something like, *I wish my staff had your enthusiasm*, or *You spend so much time here, you should work here.* Now hiring you has become the employer's idea!

4. Be politely persistent. This shows that you want to work for their company, not just get a job. To be effective, side doors often take time. Polite persistence is a hard-to-find quality valued in many jobs, and it also ensures the matter is not dropped. We learned this term from a story Juan told us. He was a natural salesman and wanted to work for one of the country's top dealerships. After several visits, he confidently asked to speak with the sales manager. He shared his success as a salesman in other industries and said he'd like to move into auto sales. The manager explained that they only hired top performers from other dealerships. Juan thanked him for his time but didn't give up. For the next week, Juan was the first person on the lot each morning and spent the next nine hours talking with the salespeople when the lot was slow, learning about the vehicles, and chatting with customers. The manager finally called him into his office and said, "If you show half as much polite persistence with my customers as you have with me, I predict you'll be one of my top salesman. I'll give you a one-month trial."

The side doors we have shown throughout the book are not the only doors. Job seekers regularly find new ways to skip the screen-out process and get noticed by the decision maker. So don't limit yourself, just make sure you use all four keys. If you do, you'll significantly increase the likelihood of being hired. If you don't, you could be wasting your time or, worse, have your side door viewed as an unsavory stunt. Remember, getting noticed because you offer something employers truly need will only impress them. Talking to the decision maker (or someone she listens to) will never be a waste of time. Allowing the employer time to figure out that he wants you makes hiring you his idea. And few expensive decisions are made quickly, so polite persistence shows you are serious about joining the team.

∞ TAKING A PAGE FROM BUSINESS . . .

Sharing "best practices" is a great way to demonstrate your abilities, establish your expertise, and help others. We invite you to share the side doors that work for you on our Wall of Side Doors at www.the6reasons.com.

Don't be discouraged if the first side door you try doesn't result in a job. They are not magic wands, just shortcuts to decision makers. You wouldn't stop sending résumés just because your first attempt, or even your tenth, didn't get you a job. Stay positive, creative, and politely persistent.

CHOOSING THE RIGHT TOOLS FOR YOU

We have given you tips for effectively using applications, résumés, cover letters, the phone, the Internet, and walk-ins to get noticed by employers. Here's a quick explanation of who should and shouldn't use each tool and why:

Applications highlight strong work history, upward progression, and job-related accomplishments. The downside is that they draw attention to many reasons employers screen out, including gaps in work history, short-term employment, criminal convictions, major illnesses, and lack of education. If you have any of these barriers, don't complete an application until after you've impressed the decision maker with your résumé or by using a side door.

Chronological résumés are preferred by most employers, but are only effective if you are staying in the field and have a strong and stable work history. If not, use a skills résumé. Both formats are significantly more effective if you emphasize accomplishments (Facts) related to your current job target rather than simply listing past responsibilities.

Skills résumés are becoming more acceptable to employers because so many people are changing fields, and they clearly show employers how your transferable skills benefit them. Under two or three major headings, list the skills and accomplishments that qualify you, and be sure employers can easily see in your Experience section where you gained each. This is easy for proof gained on past jobs—simply list the job title, company, location, and dates. For qualifications from less traditional sources, you must look at your "experience" in a new way (and get employers to also). A young woman who cared for her grandfather who had Alzheimer's listed "Personal Caregiver, Private Home, Los Angeles, CA, 8/2007 to 9/2010." Create a job title by considering the title of people who are paid to perform the same tasks. For the company, list who you did the tasks for—for example, United Way, Jackson Elementary, St. Mark's Cathedral. If you've done it for several people, list it as a small business—for example, Dan's

Web Design or Natalie's Catering. The simple heading *Experience* allows you to list unpaid qualifications. As with any proof, it must be verifiable. The young woman used her grandfather's doctor as a reference, and Dan and Natalie used "customers."

Speculative letters are a side door alternative to résumés and applications. Because they don't comfortably fit in a stack of résumés, they allow you to bypass the traditional screen-out process. Because they are addressed to the decision maker, they assure that the person with hiring power, or at least that person's gatekeeper, has the opportunity to be impressed. (Résumés sent to the decision maker are regularly redirected, unread, to HR.) The downside of effective speculative letters is that they take time to write and refine. Also, HR may resent being bypassed, though there is little they can do if the decision maker wants you on the short list.

Marketing yourself over the phone can highlight your ambition, confidence, and pleasant voice. Even if phone skills are not part of your job, it's beneficial to search using the phone because you can contact dozens of employers quickly to determine if they need your skills. The downside is that employers increasingly screen calls, so this approach requires more finesse and effort than you may have the patience for. However, it's particularly worth the effort if you wish to impress employers with your personality or skills before they meet you in person, due to a visible distraction, like an obvious disability, obesity, or age. This is not an effective tool if you have a speech impediment, strong accent, or hearing impairment, don't understand English easily, or talk very quickly, slowly, or quietly.

Walking in highlights your presentation, personality, and willingness to take action. It allows employers to see you as a person rather than a piece of paper. If your presentation and personality constitute a hard-to-find selling point, use walk-ins to market yourself for any job. They're also a quick way to get hired for jobs that require face-to-face customer contact, but only if you match the company's image and personality. The downside? If meeting you in person highlights a visible barrier or an extreme personality (shy, aggressive, depressed), use another method to approach employers initially.

Using the Internet effectively can show that you have computer skills and keep current, while saving you time and allowing employers to quickly learn a lot about you. It can also minimize a perception that you're outdated or unwilling to learn. The downside is that you can be quickly screened out if employers encounter negative information, or if you respond slowly, poorly, or inappropriately.

Which tools allow you to highlight strengths that the employer needs? Which minimize your barriers? Use the tools that do both.

In your job search journal, record your progress with each employer. Track the success of each tool, reviewing it for possible screen outs. Try each tool several times, adjusting as needed. Continue to use the tools that produce the results you want. Identify your hard-to-find quality, attitude, or skill, and craft your key message. Then, find ways to incorporate them into your various approaches. Now that you know how to look at your job search through the employer's eyes, you can develop a strategy that capitalizes on the six reasons you'll get the job.

👍 QUICK TIP

For a list of common screen outs found using the various tools and additional tips on how to use our ideas to overcome each, visit our Mini Solutions Bank at www.worknet-international .com.

Our tips, tools, and techniques have taught you how to be strategic and can make you lucky, but "luck" is *the crossroads where preparation and opportunity meet*. So you must take the time to *prepare* by:

- Discovering what the employer wants in each area of PADMAN
- Proving you can meet the employer's needs with Facts, Demonstration, Credible References, and Stories
- Removing your barriers using our six solution tools

Then create *opportunities* by using side doors. Some people do all of this instinctively, but most of us must be deliberate . . . And that is how people really get hired!

Appendix

Sample Solutions for Common Barriers

In this section we offer targeted advice to six common groups who often find it difficult to transition back into work. Notice how we have applied the tips, tools, and techniques we teach throughout the book to their issues.

 DOWNSIZED: MOVE FORWARD OR MOVE ON

If you are one of the many people who have lost their jobs because of downsizing, offshoring, or disappearing functions, you are not alone. In the last decade, many people have been forced to change fields or find new ways to use their skills. The good news is that employers are more prepared now to accept transferable skills. Here are six keys to successfully changing fields:

1. Know there are jobs out there. Thousands of people are being hired every day. Cultivate a mind-set that will help you achieve your goals. You may feel like external forces are reshaping your life, but your internal beliefs determine your attitude and actions, which in turn determine if you take a new path to hope and happiness, or get stuck.

2. Know you have options. Decide what's best for you. You can: (1) Move forward in your current field by continuing to look in your local area for related work. Use our techniques to stand out from the crowd. (2) Pursue the same work outside your local area. This may require relocating, but the Internet has made long-distance job searching easier. (3) Move on by using your current skills in a new field. If you choose a field that fascinates you, you're likely to have marketable transferable skills and knowledge. We also show you how to pull accomplishments from past jobs as well as from your hobbies, unpaid work, natural skills, personal study, and daily activities.

3. Use the skills résumé format, which highlights your transferable skills and knowledge for the new job. Remember, it's your responsibility to tell employers why you're qualified for *their* job.

4. Strategically replace terms from your former industry or activity with the vocabulary of the new industry or job.

5. Craft a good answer that explains why you're changing fields or jobs—and no, the fact that the industry has left town is not compelling enough to get you the job. Include why you have chosen the new field or job and why you chose this particular employer, as Delia does in Chapter 9.

6. Establish Credible References in the new field or for the new job. Who can vouch for your ability to fill this new position?

On average, people have three to five careers in a lifetime.[1] You don't have to pursue work from which you are repeatedly laid off out of fear that you can't do any other job. It's your life and your choice. The techniques in this book will help you move forward or move on.

 RECENT GRADUATE: I'M A WISE INVESTMENT

Congratulations! Over the course of your life, your degree will benefit you in many ways—unfortunately, it alone won't get you a job. However, along with our techniques, it can get you hired. To prove you're a wise investment, you must reduce employers' concerns about hiring you and prove you can meet their needs . . . in that order.

What might concern employers about hiring recent graduates? They enjoy learning but not working, can't apply what they've learned, spent their time partying and not learning, don't understand the demands of the business culture, lack experience but expect top dollar, or won't stay, just to name a few. Employers know there are lots of exceptions to these assumptions. You just need to prove that you're one of them. Here are seven common mistakes made by recent graduates:

1. Failing to cultivate work experience in the field before graduating. Working in the field before graduation demonstrates your passion and desire to be a part of it. You get insider information so you can identify *employer needs* in the six key areas—presentation, ability, dependability, motivation, attitude, and network—and develop proof that you understand the expectations of the business culture. If you do well, you can also gain Credible References to vouch for you and introduce you to decision makers who can hire you. It's easier to get internships, part-time jobs, and summer work as student.

2. Thinking like you, not like the employer. Employers commonly complain that recent graduates don't understand the business culture or their values. Often, this is due to a generation gap. Those running companies may be closer to your parents' age than yours, and it's reflected in their rules, expectations, and communication—for example, when your baby boomer boss says she'd like the report by 5:30 p.m., it's a polite way of saying, *Have it on my desk by 5:15.* Don't misinterpret her politeness as permission to get it done later. Generation gap or not, smart job seekers and promotable workers understand the business culture and employers' values. Many employers are willing to teach you the business culture if you prove you are eager to learn.

3. Not separating your personal and professional lives. Employers don't want you to bring your personal life to work, but they will use it to screen you out. The Internet makes it easier than ever to get information, and it's reported that 86 percent of recruiters search online to learn more about applicants.[2] Does your online image make you look like a risky investment? Screen names, photos, and information on your websites or social networking sites, who you "friend" on those sites, groups and causes you are linked with— all may be scrutinized. Employers will assume you are like the people you associate with and that this is the "real you." We help you insure your online presence and low-tech approaches help you get hired.

4. Communicating in ways that don't work for your employer and customers. Employers complain that many young professionals have replaced conversation with texting, emailing, and instant messaging. Many people who run businesses still believe that relationships require personal interaction. Before you communicate, think about your audience and goal. If you're merely passing on information, a quick email or text may work. If your goal includes making a decision, strengthening a relationship, or sharing an idea that could be enhanced with discussion, a phone call or face-to-face encounter is better. Replacing these valued interactions with brief, one-way messages in text code highlights your youth and inexperience, and can be perceived as laziness, disrespect, and a lack of professionalism.

5. Not developing mentor relationships. No one gets to the top alone. You'll get hired and advance more quickly with mentors—experts who strategically advise you on options, warn you of pitfalls, and open doors for you. Who do you know who is successful in your field? Who could you get to know? As a soon-to-be or recent graduate, you are in the perfect position to meet potential mentors. Give them a reason to like you. Show them you possess a unique quality, attitude, or skill that is worth their investment. They'll help you because your success will add to their own.

6. Thinking it's the employer's responsibility, rather than yours, to discover that you'd be good for the job. Most employers don't have the time or inclination to dig for proof that you can do the job. They expect you to discover their needs and develop clear, concise, and compelling reasons for them to consider you—and a degree and good grades are not enough. Employers judge recent graduates on passion and presentation as much as on knowledge. When hiring recent grads, they expect a significant learning curve, but are willing to make the investment to harness your enthusiasm, eagerness to impress them, current education, and willingness to work hard.

7. Job searching like everyone else. Stand out from the crowd, or you'll be screened out with the crowd. Each year, America produces 1.2 million college and university grads,[3] another 3.3 million graduates from high school,[4] and more from trade/technical schools. Posting your résumé on the Internet won't get you hired. You must search, and search differently. Get out from behind the computer, use our side doors to get to people with the power to hire you, and focus on the Hidden Market, where over 80 percent of jobs are found. Also, capitalize on your access to employers through university professors, career services, alumni, on-campus events, job fairs, visiting speakers, and internships.

If you avoid the mistakes made by so many recent grads and

use the techniques in this book, employers will see that you are a wise investment, and you'll land a job.

EXITING MILITARY: I HAVE A LOT TO OFFER, SIR!

Thank you for your service. As former military, you have a lot to offer employers—proven teamwork, time management, problem solving, handling pressure, and so much more. You may also already have the security clearance and specialized training required for some jobs. Plus, any employer can take advantage of a $4,800 tax credit[5] for hiring you. It's your job to tell employers what you have to offer. Don't expect them to figure it out for you.

To begin your transition, clarify the work you will pursue next. You have three options: (1) Look for a civilian job within the military. Your local veteran employment representative (LVER) can advise you. (2) Apply for jobs that are the civilian equivalent of your military job. Visit http://online.onetcenter.org/crosswalk to discover the civilian titles for military jobs. Find local and national companies that are military-friendly through your LVER or at www.TAOnline.com. (3) Target a job in a field that fascinates you and uses your transferable skills from the military, other work, and life. We'll show you how. Here are five tips for making your transition more successful:

1. Adapt to the civilian business culture. To be hired, you must prove you can meet the employer's needs in six key areas—presentation, ability, dependability, motivation, attitude, and network. Adapting to the differences between the military and civilian work cultures in these six areas is one of the biggest challenges you may face. For example, most civilian companies don't use formal titles. They practice *professional informality*—addressing people by their first names, smiling and maintaining friendly eye contact, and conversing in a familiar, fluid manner. Also, the posture and facial expressions used to portray strength, confidence, and respect in the military can be interpreted by civilians as rigid, aloof, or odd. To identify the cultural differences, get help from nonmilitary friends who are successful in the private sector, a military transition specialist, or a coach from your local workforce center.

2. Gather proof that you are the right person for the job. When using transferable skills from your military experience, don't assume employers understand common military terms, jobs, or rank. Transfer your military skills, education, and experience into civilian terminology so they see you as a fit for their job. Refer to fellow soldiers as *coworkers* and your commanding officers as *superiors*, *managers*, or *bosses*, and use civilian titles for your military jobs. Have people without military experience review your selling points to insure that your message is clear. Develop a skills résumé to focus on your transferable skills for the new job, rather than your past career.

3. Develop an effective network. Identify people who have successfully transitioned into the civilian workforce who can teach you the rules, act as Credible References, or mentor you through the process. Cultivate a civilian network by volunteering, participating in community or industry groups, getting involved with your child's school or activities, or joining a sports league, faith community, or hobby group. This lets you observe and get acculturated to the civilian way of life, while building a network that can help you in your job search and career development.

4. Capitalize on positive stereotypes about military personnel that are true of you—good at following instructions and completing tasks, well mannered, respectful, loyal, disciplined, hardworking, possessing a sense of duty, and so forth. Many businesses feel compelled to hire and train veterans, so maximize this opportunity. And prepare to combat negative stereotypes about hiring ex-military personnel—too rigid and intimidating, post-traumatic stress, lack creative thinking or personal initiative, or have a sense of entitlement because of the sacrifice made. Present yourself, in words and actions, as an exception to these stereotypes, as Sergeant Murphy does in Chapter 8.

5. Use available military transition services—the GI Bill, the Reserve Educational Assistance Program, veteran scholarships, and the military transitional assistance programs. Visit www.gibill.va.gov for more information.

We wish you the best of luck as you set out on this new adventure.

ECONOMIC IMMIGRANT: WORKING FOR A BETTER LIFE

If you have uprooted yourself and your family and moved to a new country, you're hoping to create a better life, and work is essential. It's challenging to find work in a new country, even if you speak the language, have the legal right to work, and have good education and experience from your own country. But millions of economic immigrants have successfully made the transition,[6] and you can, too. Here are the three major challenges, and tips for overcoming them:

1. Qualifications. Credentials, degrees, licenses, and certifications you gained outside your new country may not be recognized. You can find information online about re-credentialing programs that may help you use your credentials in your new country, though you may be required to reinvest in a majority of your education. Another option is to pursue nonlicensed or lower-level jobs in your field for which employers would love to have someone with your skill level. And for any job that doesn't require a credential, employers can hire you once they test and confirm your knowledge and skills.

2. Cultural differences. There will be important differences between your previous business culture and that of your new country. Not understanding these differences can get you screened out. Employers judge you not only on your vocational skills, but in six key areas—presentation, ability, dependability, motivation, attitude, and network. As we share in this book, employers have a unique definition of each. You have two options, you can: socialize and work primarily with people from your home culture, or you can become *bicultural* and work in the local business culture. Becoming bicultural means that when you're in your home culture you use its language and rules, and when you're working you speak business English and follow the rules of the local business culture. The easiest way to learn a new business culture is to find a mentor who is successful in it and will teach you. You can also observe how employer expectations are similar or different from your home culture, and discuss it with employers, a local friend, or your mentor, as Yoku does in Chapter 11.

3. The process. The process of job searching and interviewing will be different than in your previous culture. Have a mentor walk you through it. Look for the subtle differences in protocol. Verify what is meant by each bullet point on a job description. Review the type of questions that will be asked, and use Chapter 16 to help craft your answers. In the United States, interviewers expect you to share all the best things you offer, and perhaps even exaggerate slightly, so always put your best foot forward. If your home culture values humility, so you humbly share less than your best because you don't want to brag, you will likely to be screened out. Learn to confidently share your key message (top three to six selling points) throughout each interview.

In this book we share many specific examples of the rules for the Western business culture, so you can compare it to your own. We also share stories of how other people have successfully made the transition. When someone enters your home culture and doesn't follow the rules, you notice. If that person makes an effort to adopt your customs, you notice, and are more gracious if he unknowingly breaks rules. The same is true in our business culture.

♿ DISABILITY: PLEASE JUDGE ME ON MY ABILITY

Almost half of all working-age people with disabilities in America today are employed. That's nearly 20 million people,[7] and you can join them. Everyone has strengths and weaknesses, and all of us make accommodations at work for our limitations. However, if you have a disability, it can overshadow your talents and make employers think it's too disruptive or costly to accommodate you. The Americans with Disabilities Act (ADA) is designed to decrease employment discrimination against qualified individuals with disabilities,[8] but it doesn't require employers to hire you. As with any candidate, employers will choose you because you prove you can solve a problem, make them money, or help them be more successful. But you must also prove your disability will not become their problem. Use the strategies in this book and the five tips below to avoid getting screened out, and to get hired:

1. Target jobs you are fully qualified to do with your disability so the focus is on your abilities, not your limitations. This will also lay the foundation to request a reasonable accommodation from the employer who hires you. If you are unsure what you are qualified to do, visit your local workforce center (www.servicelocator.org), conduct a skills search at http://online.onetcenter.org, or join an online community designed to support people with your disability, and ask for suggestions.

2. Structure your job search so employers see your value *before* they notice your disability, as we teach in Chapter 19. If you have a visible disability, market yourself on paper, the Internet, or the phone. When you are invited to interview in person, call back to discuss the details and initiate an informal phone interview by asking questions about the position and sharing your unique selling points for the job, so the employer begins to see what they gain in hiring you before they meet you. If you have an auditory disability, there are smart phones and software that offer video relay service, or allow you to read on your mobile phone what others are saying, before you respond in your own voice. Sprint and other companies offer free services for their technology.[9] If your disability is not visible, market yourself with methods that play to your strengths and show that you meet the employer's needs. In all cases, use the side doors we teach to highlight your abilities and minimize your disability.

3. Decide whether and how to disclose your disability. You're not obligated to disclose it, before or after you're hired. However, if employers are likely to notice it, address it up front as David does in Chapter 15. If it's not noticeable but employers may discover it, share it after they make the job offer but before you accept. This insures that you're evaluated based on your ability, but the employer doesn't feel deceived later.

4. Avoid words and imagery that could intensify employer concerns. "Accommodation" becomes *resource that will make me most productive for you*, "deafness" becomes *hard of hearing*, "missing hand" becomes *one fully functioning hand*, and *issue* or *my situation* are safe catch-alls for "disability."

5. Reduce the employer's perceived risk. If you can, before your job search, invest in the resources needed to make you more productive. Accommodations can be very simple—a special pillow for your back, a fan to cool the air, a quiet spot to work, or a lamp instead of fluorescent lighting. If you can't afford it, research options and, once hired, discuss solutions with HR. If you require significant accommodation to work at the site, you might negotiate working from home or via the Internet. Also, there are programs and advocates that can help an employer carve out a job that allows you to do just the tasks you can do well.

Having solutions to eliminate employers' concerns is the key to refocusing them on your abilities, and getting hired.

CRIMINAL CONVICTION: IF YOU TAKE THE RISK, YOU WON'T BE SORRY

Currently, more than one in every thirty-one Americans is on probation, in jail, in prison, or on parole.[10] Many more have criminal convictions in their past. If you do, you are not alone, but you may believe that employers won't give you a second chance. A study in Los Angeles showed that 55 percent of employers are willing to consider people with convictions.[11] Hundreds of thousands of ex-offenders are working today, many in great jobs. And no, they did not have to lie to get the job. You must give employers a reason to believe you won't commit a crime again, and prove that your skills, attitudes, and qualities make you worth the risk. The real challenge is getting past the screen-out process so you can tell your side of the story. Here are four proven tips:

1. Choose your job carefully. Target jobs you are allowed to do, companies that don't have policies against hiring people with convictions, and employers who believe in second chances and are more sympathetic toward your issue (as described in Chapter 18). Often, small and midsize companies are more willing to listen and give you a second chance. Ask friends, community advocates, employment workers, or parole officers if they know where other ex-offenders have been hired.

2. Gather evidence that you have changed. Develop and

share new friends, activities, and attitudes that paint a positive picture of your life today, and create connections with Credible References who can vouch for the change.

3. Avoid job applications. They are the least effective tool for ex-offenders because you must answer questions about convictions before you can prove your value. Use a skills résumé, like Deborah's (shown on page 229), and our side door techniques. When you must complete an application, read the questions carefully.

- If they ask about felony convictions, then the answer regarding arrests, misdemeanors, or trials that did not result in felony convictions is simply no.
- If they ask about arrests, even if you've been arrested but never convicted, answer this as you would any other illegal question—"N/A" for Not Applicable.
- If you were convicted of the type of crime they asked about, write, "Will explain in the interview" without additional details. Your application becomes part of your personnel file and you don't want staff discovering the details, plus details can scare off employers. That said, you might choose to list and minimize the conviction—for example, *More than 20 years ago* or *Misdemeanor*, or list your milder offenses, such as *traffic violation, public protest, DUI—no longer drink*, and *Will explain in interview*—so employers realize it's not as bad as they assumed.
- If you have a juvenile conviction and are now over eighteen, the courts should have sealed your record, allowing you to legally answer no. If the record hasn't been sealed, write *As a juvenile—will explain in interview.*
- If you're unsure of the details, contact each county in which you offended to access your official record. Get help from a community advocate, local workforce

center, or websites such as www.criminalsearches
.com.

4. Use a skills résumé. It allows you to control the information given. Take a look at Deborah's résumé on the next page. If you were an employer hiring an administrative assistant, would you interview her?

If you would interview her, you think like many employers. Deborah's résumé clearly tells employers why she is qualified for the job. Did it occur to you that during her experience with CDCR (California Department of Corrections and Rehabilitation), she was an inmate? It didn't occur to employers. The heading *Experience* allowed her to include her prison work along with her previous employment to prove she meets the employer's needs. A great résumé alone can't get you the job, but it can give you a chance to share your good answer. Use the process in Chapter 16 to craft a good answer that increases your confidence and shows employers that what they'll gain from hiring you outweighs the risks.

Deborah planned to share her good answer before the end of the first interview, because she didn't want employers to discover her conviction when they called the prison for a reference.

➥ DID YOU KNOW?

Employers have a legal right to ask about criminal convictions. Don't lie; it can get you fired later. Use our techniques to show employers your value before explaining your background. If you're offered a job before it comes up, follow Deborah's example below and share your good answer before accepting the job. It will save you from always looking over your shoulder, and most employers will respect your honesty.

DEBORAH R. JOHNSON

Riverside, CA   951.555.5786
djohnson@aol.com   www.Linked.com/in/DeborahRJohnson

OBJECTIVE: Administrative assistant in a small, fast-growing business

SUMMARY OF QUALIFICATIONS

- More than 10 years of office and computer experience.
- Helped manage and grow a successful, family-run business.
- Proven ability to manage multiple tasks at once.
- Computer literacy, including MS Office, MS Access, QuickBooks, and the Internet.
- Excellent attendance: Missed only 8 days in 10 years.

Office Skills

- Task Management: Enjoy managing multiple tasks. Known by colleagues as organized and efficient.
- Customer Service: Received 3 "outstanding" ratings for customer service in the last 5 years.
- Phone Skills: Pleasant phone voice with proven ability to handle multi-line phone system.
- Filing: Competent in designing, organizing, and maintaining physical and computerized filing systems.
- Data Entry: Typing speed of 60 wpm and 10-key by touch.
- Business Correspondence: Proficient in business correspondence, including excellent spelling, grammar, and punctuation.
- Bookkeeping: Experienced in maintaining petty cash and expense reports. Proficient in QuickBooks, and can quickly learn other programs. Proven success in basic accounts receivable and payable, and collecting on outstanding invoices, while maintaining customers.

- Travel Arrangements: Effective at booking hotels, air and ground transportation, and managing mileage and perks accounts.
- Special Projects: Enjoy event planning, special projects, contributing to the company newsletter.

Computer Skills

- Computer Literate: Know 5 computer programs, learn quickly, and can use manuals effectively.
- Computer Technology: Capable of basic computer upgrades including adding modems, memory, sound and VGA cards, loading software, and troubleshooting basic software and hardware problems.
- Internet: More than 5 years experience researching and communicating on the Internet.

EXPERIENCE

Computerized Learning Center Assistant, CDCR	2002–2010
Office Assistant, CDRC	2000–2001
Office Manager/Partner, Johnson Plumbing	1985–1999

EDUCATION

Computer training in MS Office Professional Suite and Access
Independent study in MS Access and QuickBooks
Course work including typing, filing, business correspondence and terminology, and shorthand

DEBORAH R. JOHNSON

djohnson@aol.com   951.555.5786

When asked about her work with CDCR, Deborah shared stories and facts about her accomplishments at the learning center, then . . . *Before we move on, I'd like to share the rest of the story about my time with CDCR. It's personal, but I think you have the right to know. When I was very young, I married a man who became violent. When it started to hurt my children, I knew we had to get out. He said he'd kill us if we tried, and I believed him. I felt I had no choice but to act first, and that brought me to CDCR. I will never forget the look in my daughters' eyes when they realized I couldn't come home with them. I made a vow, then and there, to make it up to them. At CDCR, I got counseling and discovered other options I hadn't seen at the time. And I was given the opportunity to become a trusted member of the Learning Center team, where I gained many of the skills you see on my résumé, and was able to help a lot of other women gain the skills they need to start their lives over again. Today, my life is very different. I love being with my girls and have the support of great friends. I know my story may have come as a surprise, and it may feel risky to give me a second chance. But I promise that if you do, I'll be your most loyal and hardworking employee. I will never take this chance for granted. Plus, as you said earlier, I have the skills you are looking for and I am focused on adding to your success.*

Deborah's résumé got her the interview, but her good answer, skills, and positive attitude got her the job!

SAMPLE PADMAN PLAN	1. Job Target	
	2. Employer Needs	**3. My Proof** Facts, Story, Demonstration, Credible Reference
P Presentation	• • • •	☐ Facts ☐ Story ☐ Demo ☐ CR _____ ☐ Facts ☐ Story ☐ Demo ☐ CR _____ ☐ Facts ☐ Story ☐ Demo ☐ CR _____ ☐ Facts ☐ Story ☐ Demo ☐ CR _____
A Ability	• • • •	☐ Facts ☐ Story ☐ Demo ☐ CR _____ ☐ Facts ☐ Story ☐ Demo ☐ CR _____ ☐ Facts ☐ Story ☐ Demo ☐ CR _____ ☐ Facts ☐ Story ☐ Demo ☐ CR _____
D Dependability	• • • •	☐ Facts ☐ Story ☐ Demo ☐ CR _____ ☐ Facts ☐ Story ☐ Demo ☐ CR _____ ☐ Facts ☐ Story ☐ Demo ☐ CR _____ ☐ Facts ☐ Story ☐ Demo ☐ CR _____
M Motivation	• • • •	☐ Facts ☐ Story ☐ Demo ☐ CR _____ ☐ Facts ☐ Story ☐ Demo ☐ CR _____ ☐ Facts ☐ Story ☐ Demo ☐ CR _____ ☐ Facts ☐ Story ☐ Demo ☐ CR _____
A Attitude	• • • •	☐ Facts ☐ Story ☐ Demo ☐ CR _____ ☐ Facts ☐ Story ☐ Demo ☐ CR _____ ☐ Facts ☐ Story ☐ Demo ☐ CR _____ ☐ Facts ☐ Story ☐ Demo ☐ CR _____
N Network	• • • •	☐ Facts ☐ Story ☐ Demo ☐ CR _____ ☐ Facts ☐ Story ☐ Demo ☐ CR _____ ☐ Facts ☐ Story ☐ Demo ☐ CR _____ ☐ Facts ☐ Story ☐ Demo ☐ CR _____

SAMPLE PADMAN PLAN	4. MyBarriers	5. Solution Tools Learn a New Skill * Access a Resource * Change Your Job Target * Adjust Your Outlook * Adjust the Employer's Perception * Craft a Good Answer
P Presentation	• • •	☐ Skill ☐ Resource ☐ Target ☐ Outlook ☐ Perception ☐ GA ☐ Skill ☐ Resource ☐ Target ☐ Outlook ☐ Perception ☐ GA ☐ Skill ☐ Resource ☐ Target ☐ Outlook ☐ Perception ☐ GA
A Ability	• • •	☐ Skill ☐ Resource ☐ Target ☐ Outlook ☐ Perception ☐ GA ☐ Skill ☐ Resource ☐ Target ☐ Outlook ☐ Perception ☐ GA ☐ Skill ☐ Resource ☐ Target ☐ Outlook ☐ Perception ☐ GA
D Dependability	• • •	☐ Skill ☐ Resource ☐ Target ☐ Outlook ☐ Perception ☐ GA ☐ Skill ☐ Resource ☐ Target ☐ Outlook ☐ Perception ☐ GA ☐ Skill ☐ Resource ☐ Target ☐ Outlook ☐ Perception ☐ GA
M Motivation	• • •	☐ Skill ☐ Resource ☐ Target ☐ Outlook ☐ Perception ☐ GA ☐ Skill ☐ Resource ☐ Target ☐ Outlook ☐ Perception ☐ GA ☐ Skill ☐ Resource ☐ Target ☐ Outlook ☐ Perception ☐ GA
A Attitude	• • •	☐ Skill ☐ Resource ☐ Target ☐ Outlook ☐ Perception ☐ GA ☐ Skill ☐ Resource ☐ Target ☐ Outlook ☐ Perception ☐ GA ☐ Skill ☐ Resource ☐ Target ☐ Outlook ☐ Perception ☐ GA
N Network	• • •	☐ Skill ☐ Resource ☐ Target ☐ Outlook ☐ Perception ☐ GA ☐ Skill ☐ Resource ☐ Target ☐ Outlook ☐ Perception ☐ GA ☐ Skill ☐ Resource ☐ Target ☐ Outlook ☐ Perception ☐ GA

Notes

INTRODUCTION

1 In January 2009, the U.S. government reported that more than 700,000 people had lost their jobs, that 4.3 million people had found jobs, and that more than 1 million vacancies remained unfilled.

1. THINKING LIKE EVERYONE ELSE CAN KEEP YOU UNEMPLOYED

1 States determine the ratio of job seekers to job openings by comparing the number of registered job seekers to a retrospective estimate of the number of jobs available. Jobs available are based on new employees added to company's payroll. The percentage of unpublicized job opportunities results because many of the jobs filled were never listed in their state's job opening database. Therefore, 20 percent of jobs in the Open Market and 80 percent of jobs in the Hidden Market are the accepted industry averages.

2 *Getting a Job*, 2nd ed., by Mark Granovetter, published in 1995 by the University of Chicago Press.

3 *The Tipping Point*, by Malcolm Gladwell, published in 2000 by Back Bay Books/Little, Brown and Company, chapter 2.4.

2. THE HIRING PROCESS THROUGH
THE EMPLOYER'S EYES

1 *What Color Is Your Parachute? A Practical Manual for Job-Hunters and Career-Changers*, "Hard Times" ed., by Richard Bolles, published in 2009 by Ten Speed Press. This is the bestselling job-hunting and career-changing book in the world.

3. PADMAN—THE 6 REASONS YOU ARE HIRED
OR SCREENED OUT

1 "2008 Executive Job Market Intelligence Report" from ExecuNet, www.execunet.com.

5. STAND OUT FROM THE CROWD BY GIVING FACTS

1 Scott A. Shane. "Are Medium-Size Businesses the Job Creators?" *New York Times*, August 5, 2009, http://boss.blogs.nytimes.com/2009/08/05/are-medium-sized-businesses-the-job-creators.

7. STAND OUT FROM THE CROWD BY OFFERING
CREDIBLE REFERENCES

1 See *The Tipping Point* (page 235).

8. STAND OUT FROM THE CROWD
BY TELLING STORIES

1 For more information, see Quintessential Careers' online article "STAR Interviewing Response Technique for Success in Behavioral Job Interviews" at www.quintcareers.com/STAR_interviewing.html.

2 See *What Color Is Your Parachute?* (page 235).

11. SOLUTION TOOL 1: LEARN A NEW SKILL

1 *Did You Know? 3.0: Globalization & The Information Age*, rev. ed., created by Karl Fisch and modified by Scott McLeod. Video available at www .youtube.com/9nmUB2qls.

2 The neurolinguistic programming (NLP) variation on Neil Fleming's VARK model is one of the most widely used learning models. See http:// en.wikipedia.org/wiki/Learning_styles.

3 Learn more about the three learning styles and take a quick test to determine your learning style at http://people.usd.edu/~bwjames/tut/learning-style.

13. SOLUTION TOOL 3: CHANGE YOUR JOB TARGET

1 *The Dictionary of Occupational Titles* was the creation of the Employment and Training Administration of the U.S. Department of Labor, which used its thousands of occupational definitions to match job seekers to jobs from 1939 to the late 1990s. Last revised and produced in 1991, it offered details on 12,740 job titles. It has been replaced by O*Net at http://online.onetcenter.org.

14. SOLUTION TOOL 4: ADJUST YOUR OUTLOOK

1 Daniel Porot is one of Europe's leading pioneers in career design and job hunting. Learn more at www.porot.com/en/home.

17. OVERCOMING YOUR BARRIERS

1 WorkNet Publications, www.worknet-international.com.

PART 4. CREATING AN EFFECTIVE JOB SEARCH STRATEGY

1 See *What Color Is Your Parachute?* (page 235).

19. CHOOSING THE STRATEGY THAT'S BEST FOR YOU

1 Based on the work of Italian economist Vilfredo Pareto, who in 1906 created a mathematical formula to describe the unequal distribution of wealth in his country, observing that 20 percent of the people owned 80 percent of the wealth. In the United States in the 1930s and '40s, Quality Management pioneer Dr. Joseph Juran recognized a universal principle that 20 percent of something is always responsible for 80 percent of the results. This Pareto's Principle or the 80/20 Rule means that in anything a few (20 percent) are vital and many (80 percent) are trivial.

APPENDIX

1 According to the U.S. Department of Labor, the average U.S. worker changes careers three to five times during his or her lifetime.

2 See "2008 Executive Job Market Intelligence Report" (page 236).

3 According to the National Center for Education Statistics (http://nces.ed .gov/programs/coe/2009/section3/table-dcd-1.asp), 1,524,092 bachelor's degrees and 728,114 associate's degrees were bestowed in 2009.

4 According to the National Center for Education Statistics (http://nces .ed.gov/programs/digest/d08/), about 3,328,000 high school students were expected to graduate during the 2008–2009 school year.

5 Companies that a hire a military veteran who has served on active duty within the past five years may be eligible to receive a $4,800 tax credit for each veteran hired. For details, visit www.taonline.com/employers/ registerform.asp.

6 According to the U.S. Census Bureau's 2008 American Community Survey, there were 37,960,935 foreign born in the United States.

7 According to the Survey of Income and Program Participation (SIPP), 32.1 million working-age people have a disability. Of them, 82.1 percent of people without a disability are employed, 76.9 percent of people with a nonsevere disability are employed, and 26.1 percent of people with a severe disability are employed (www.infouse.com/disabilitydata/workdisability/1_1.php).

8 The Americans with Disabilities Act of 1990 prohibits private employers, state and local governments, employment agencies, and labor unions from discriminating against qualified individuals with disabilities in job application procedures, hiring, firing, advancement, compensation, job training, and other terms, conditions, and privileges of employment. The ADA covers employers with fifteen or more employees, including state and local governments. It also applies to employment agencies and to labor organizations (www.eeoc.gov/facts/fs-ada.html).

9 The Federal Communications Commission has approved funding for video relay service through the Interstate Telecommunications Relay Services Fund. The cost of the high-speed Internet and telephone service is the responsibility of the user. Learn more about Sprint resources at www.sprintrelay.com/webcaptel_go.htm.

10 According to the Bureau of Justice Statistics (http://bjs.ojp.usdoj.gov/index.cfm?ty=tp&tid=11), an estimated 5.6 million American adults had been imprisoned at some point in 2001. The *Total Correctional Population* states that in 2008 more than 7.3 million people were on probation, in jail or prison, or on parole at year's end—3.2 percent of all U.S. adult residents or 1 in every 31 adults.

11 According to the National Poverty Center, Gerald R. Ford School of Public Policy, University of Michigan's *Effect of an Applicant's Criminal History on Employer Hiring Decisions and Screening Practices* paper (December 2004), 619 organizations in Los Angeles were surveyed in 2001 and respondents were asked whether they would accept an applicant with a criminal record for the last job they had available that did not require a college degree. 5.3 percent definitely would, 15.7 percent probably would, and for another 35.4 percent it would depend on the crime (www.usatoday.com/money/economy/employment/2003-11-21-workers_x.htm).

Index

Page numbers in *italics* represent charts.

About the Authors

Debra Angel MacDougall is the founder and president of WorkNet International Inc. She and her associates devote their time to assisting government and private organizations throughout North America, Australia, New Zealand, and the United Kingdom to develop effective career development/job placement programs for individuals who are finding it difficult to get good jobs.

She has received recognition for her inspired and practical response to social issues over the last twenty-five years, including Outstanding Young Woman presented by the United Nations' National Council of Women—USA, the National Customer Service Award presented by the National Association of Workforce Development Professionals, and Woman of the Year presented by the Salvation Army. She is the coauthor of the highly acclaimed book *No One Is Unemployable: Creative Solutions for Overcoming Barriers to Employment*, named a Top Ten Career Book of the Year by the *Los Angeles Times*, and was named by Richard Bolles, author of *What Color Is Your Parachute?*, as one of "six thinkers who have had the most influence on me, over the years." She lives in Scotland with her husband, Gordon.

Elisabeth Harney Sanders-Park is certified as a job and career transition coach and workforce development professional, and has greatly influenced the field of career development for the last fifteen years. She is a nationally recognized tough career transitions expert and a highly sought-after trainer, consultant, and keynote speaker. She coauthored the acclaimed book *No One Is Unemployable* as well as other widely used industry-leading resources and is a regular columnist for "The Career Planning & Adult Development Network" newsletter. She has been a guest expert on radio shows, television news, and talk shows, including *Rikki Lake, Extra! Australia*, and *American Family*.

She is the president of WorkNet Solutions, which exists to help improve the effectiveness of North American government and private organizations to successfully transition people with significant barriers into the workforce. Her customers include welfare-to-work systems, recovery programs, colleges and universities, correctional programs, vocational training schools, refugee and relocation services, and others. She and her husband, Brian, live with their three children in North Carolina.